HAPPY GREAT DAY®
SELF-CARE HABITS

To Create A Beautiful Life

SUZANA WARD

Foreword By Pamela G. Gaudry, MD
International Pioneer On Intimacy & Emotional Resilience

Paperback ISBN: 979-8-9994456-0-5
Hardcover ISBN: 979-8-9994456-1-2

Printed in the United States of America.

TABLE OF CONTENTS

PRAISE FOR HAPPY GREAT DAY®

"Trust me, the chapter 'Can You Afford Those Over-The-Knee-Go-Go Boots?' will pay for this book many times over. As Suzana's close friend and trusty accountant, it's been a delight to share my top-notch, easy financial hacks for women with her. I teach clients to treat a self-audit like an exciting treasure hunt! Suzana and I have laughed (and cried) about the sneaky drains on her wallet. After reading *Happy Great Day®: Self-Care Habits to Create a Beautiful Life,* you'll be laughing all the way to the bank."

~ Rose Pitt, Principal
Jerry Mcnair Accounting Firm
Savannah, Georgia

"This book was a revelation for me, and a reminder to recapture my joy. I especially related to the chapter that talked about how wearing pretty, little undies can make you feel sexy and confident all day. My sister has rooted around in my laundry and said, 'I don't get it, why do you buy these frilly little things, no one sees them.' And I say, 'first of all, you don't know who sees them, and second, because I see them, and they make me feel pretty.' When I read that chapter, I literally said, 'Yes! Exactly!' out loud and nearly scared my cats half to death. There were also chapters with amazing tips and suggestions for things I had not done or considered before, but I certainly will now."

~ Melissa B. Kendrick
Savannah, Georgia

"This book contains foundational principles in some of the most important pillars of life: self-image, friendships, romantic relationships, professional success, sense of belonging and safety, physical fitness, finances, and physical and spiritual nourishment. By encouraging visualization of positive changes, *Happy Great Day® Self-Care Habits To Create A Beautiful Life* will shift your mindset into one of growth and elegance. Halfway through reading this book, I took three hours to write down and visualize everything I want in every area of my life. By the time I finished the book, some of my visualizations were already taking shape in the real world."

~ Kathryn Schroeder
Denver, Colorado

DEDICATION

A woman with "grit" embraces setbacks as "experience" and courageously pushes forward toward better circumstances in her darkest hours. This book was inspired by the wildest desires of remarkable women, whom I affectionately call "Guardian Gals™," or "GGs."

I want to give special thanks to my GG since childhood, Dr. Pamela G. Gaudry.

Here's an excerpt from a text I sent to her on December 24, 2022:

Dear Friend!

Thank you for pulling me back from a sad ending during our last office visit. I vividly remember screaming and telling God to f*** off as I shot an emphatic bird at the ceiling. You must have heard me sobbing loudly and gulping for air as I raced out of your door. Your waiting room was packed with wide-eyed, shocked patients who sat frozen after overhearing my rant.

It would have been understandable if you had thrown me out on the street, but, instead, you reacted with unexpected compassion that saved my life. The last time I saw you, I was hurting, frightened, and tethered to heavy, gray sadness. I now realize that on that unforgettably painful day in your office when you responded to my tantrum with a long hug, God was holding me in his arms *through you*.

FOREWORD
HAPPY GREAT DAY®
SELF-CARE HABITS TO
CREATE A BEAUTIFUL LIFE

Pamela G. Gaudry, MD

International Pioneer On Intimacy and Emotional Resilience
OB/GYN, Intimacy Counselor, and Menopause Specialist
Founder of The Georgia Center for Menopausal Medicine and Direct Primary Care
Author of *Love, Sweat and Tears: The Menopause Romance Revolution*

It all started with a call. I heard that happy and excited voice on the other end, and in an instant, I wondered how Suzana was doing and where she was living. I've known her for over 45 years, and over the years we've reconnected time after time, always picking up right where we left off just like great friends do. The last time we spoke she was "embracing an adventure." I heard her smile through the sound waves when I answered the phone. She told me she had written a book, asked if I'd write the foreword, and mentioned she planned to write more in the next year.

9

Happy Great Day®. I thought long and hard about the title of her book. If you know Suzana, you know that this title is perfect for her. Does it resonate with you? Does it make sense? Do you wake up each day, knowing it will be a happy great day®? Sometimes I do, but if I'm being honest, most of the time, I wish I could just stay in bed and ignore the day. I don't know what it will bring. In fact, I often expect things to go wrong.

Then I read Suzana's book. I dove in without any preconceived notions. I didn't expect it to "change my life." I simply wanted to give it my full attention and honor it, as it deserved. When I finally carved out time to read, I wished that I had done so sooner. I couldn't put it down and finished the entire book in one sitting.

I've had the pleasure of watching Suzana grow from an awkward teenager into the beautiful, powerful woman she is today. We've shared many trials and tribulations, and through it all, I've had the privilege of being her friend, confidant, physician, and counselor. Each role has been treasured, and each experience has deepened my admiration for her.

She possesses a unique sense of commitment and dedication to her family and friends—qualities that are rare in this world. Anyone whose life she touches is forever changed by her infectious energy, grace, and way of making others feel seen. Since reading this book, I've made a few changes in my life:

- I accept help from my friends when they volunteer their time because I've learned that engaging in shared experiences, particularly during tough situations, strengthens emotional bonds. Accepting assistance fosters a sense of reciprocity, making *both of us* feel valued and appreciated.
- I tell people how much they mean to me and how much their positive impact matters in my life.

- I'm making a greater effort to give back to "my squad" and trying to spread smiles—even to strangers.
- I'm planning a gourmet picnic with wine and cheese for a close friend, embracing silliness and allowing myself to laugh freely and loudly.
- I'm decorating my space to make it cozy and *mine*, and I'm more consciously trying to eat well and exercise.
- I'm identifying my Guardian Gals™ and keeping them close.

And most importantly, I wake up each day and make a more conscious attempt to expect things to go right.

INTRODUCTION

This book is for the woman who needs to:

- stop apologizing and embrace her goddess energy;
- reclaim her sexuality; and
- find enough free time to take a nap, apply some eyeliner, and start a load of laundry.

If you're an adventure-seeker craving a more meaningful and exciting life, buckle up! These invaluable strategies for unshakeable confidence under fire are your call to action. The diverse contributors to this work—our inspiring Guardian Gals™ (GGs)—are team players who refuse to be manipulated or controlled. They research, connect, and strategically plan to win their battles without a fight. If suggestions from these fearless trailblazers feel light-years from your comfort zone, that's a sign that you're in for a treat: the benefit of new and creative perspectives. After all, no sophisticated, busy woman would settle for a mundane approach to planning her Happy Great Day®.

One of the joys of embracing self-acceptance is showing up to have fun rather than seeking approval. This is what I encourage you to do in this book: Chapter 1 shares an example of how to picture a happier home life, and Chapter 2 challenges you to explore feeling both treasured and desired in your love life. Discover "sexy chromotherapy" in Chapter 6, and in Chapter 16, a workout that will give you the exhilarating freedom of a self-assured, bold, and dazzling bird soaring straight toward the sun. Chapter 19 features a composite character who aches for your patience and understanding. You may recognize her in the mirror.

As my quest to learn self-care skills intensified, I left my comfort zone and initiated conversations and brief interviews with intriguing strangers and prominent community members. The female mail carrier, who is always smiling, said yes to lunch, and I struck up a discussion with a vivacious travel blogger who lived for daring adventures. I asked my optician to meet for coffee, and I chatted with a colorful group of tattoo artists seated across from me in my favorite park.

No one can guarantee how tomorrow will unfold, but this material can provide engaging strategies for feeling more glamorous, joyful, and kissable. Some sections will resonate more than others. Instead of judging or copying this advice, allow the mistakes and victories of other women to help you customize the keys to your happiness, and consult a licensed professional before attempting any techniques introduced here.

As you turn the page, take what resonates, laugh at what doesn't, and leave the rest. This isn't a rulebook, it's a permission slip to be curious, to play, to question, to rest, to roar, and to remember that your pleasure, power, and peace are not luxuries; they're your birthright. Let this book be your companion as you rediscover the wild, wise, and worthy woman within.

Many of the individuals I spoke with entrusted me with secrets that I vowed to safeguard with my life. Therefore, any first-person narrative, use of "I" and "my" or stories that appear to be from the author's perspective, reflect a blended voice of shared experiences. Essentially, quotes are attributed to a fictionalized narrator resembling me. To shield GGs from unwanted attention, I also added other stories to my own, used nicknames and modified contributors' identifying details in the creation of composite characters.

This work merges narratives that are themes among women. All accounts and perspectives were presented to the author as authentic, but it is impossible to ensure accuracy in a book about manifesting women's unleashed fantasies.

xoxo Surzaha

Chapter 1

HARNESS THE POWER OF POSITIVE VISUALIZATION TO GET YOUR LIFE ON TRACK

SYNOPSIS:

Considering destinations where you might have an easier life makes sense amid news of unpredictable weather disasters impacting cities worldwide. Let your imagination run wild as you indulge in visions of what might be a paradise for you.

Alternatively, if you long for a fresh start, but can't envision a physical move, why not elevate your current space with wallet-friendly, luxurious enhancements that transform your home into a captivating retreat?

Even though Mom was terminally ill, we couldn't contain our excitement as we packed our bags and raced to Colorado to acquire emergency access to specialty medical care for her. She passed away shortly after we arrived. But we shared amazing, unforgettable memories in the magical, snowy mountains. Our mutual goals were finding basic amenities and losing ourselves in nature's healing power. We envisioned road trips along winding trails way up in the plush, green, high country. We also wanted a vibrant art scene, proximity to a pharmacy, and an airport.

How did we decide on Colorado? The first step was searching for affordable and comfortable outdoor communities online. Plenty of free websites and apps can help you locate and compare the features of individual neighborhoods. It's possible to kick back in an armchair and explore new-to-you areas where the lifestyle is an upbeat, sophisticated experience, the economy is robust, the housing is luxurious and less expensive, and the crime rate is lower.

Olivia, a friend I made through a grief and loss support group, described herself as having been stuck in the same rut for many years. She called the numbness caused by post-traumatic stress "Mother Nature's big hug." With a kind and gentle voice, Olivia shared, "Not feeling anything at all whatsoever allowed me to avoid facing incomprehensible sadness."

She also noted that, despite her athletic background and lean, fit body, staying on the rollercoaster of panic for too many years had severely impacted her health. Olivia recounted the shock and fear she experienced when she felt a sudden, complete loss of physical and mental energy.

"I needed to be numb for a while," my new friend recalled. "My brain was overloaded and claimed time to heal itself. I had worked so hard and planned so hard but never played. Then, one day, everything I had worked for went away. Poof! All the people I treasured were gone, and all my dreams crashed down around me. There was safety in that big hug of numbness."

Olivia was referred to the Motivation Counselor, a retired nurse who left her career working in a memory care facility for seniors to become a stress management counselor. The Motivation Counselor told Olivia that she would help her solve her physical issues by using "positivity exercises." My new friend explained that she was instructed to post upbeat goals in a prominent place in her home. "Every time I marked off a goal, I felt a surge of accomplishment," she said. She proudly noted that she no longer sees the counselor "because I've learned to do self-guided positive visualization myself."

Olivia added, "I've defined my primary goal and hit that target to feel lighthearted and experience more pleasure." Indeed, she had achieved more than that, given that she also stated:

- "Now I get to help people in a work-from-anywhere career I love."
- "'Home' is a comforting place where I grow edible violas and pansies in my backyard."
- "My backside is rock-hard, and my biceps are made of steel. I've even started training for my first 24K race and will travel the world to compete in thrilling marathon destinations."

As I listened to Olivia share her victories, I realized how much I wanted my own droopy backside to become rock-hard and for my wimpy arms to pack steel biceps. After we hung up, I contacted the Motivation Counselor and requested a private session.

Two weeks later, in our online video meeting, the counselor asked me to tell her about my background before she struck a blow to my soul.

"What I'm about to say is going to be difficult for you to hear," she stated, crinkling her nose slightly. "Your problem is that while you have a place to sleep at night, it lacks the warmth and nurturing relationships that make it a 'home.'" My counselor gestured with her fingers to indicate quotation marks around the word home.

"Your house sounds like a burden because you obsess about the associated financial strain and maintenance issues," she continued. By contrast, a home should feel like a refuge from life's stress, representing comfort, belonging, and security. It's where memories are created, relationships are nurtured, and individuals can truly be themselves. A home is a sanctuary filled with love, laughter, and personal history, offering a sense of peace and identity."

"It also sounds like your house is filled with impersonal, generic décor and furnishings, whereas a home can be defined by thoughtful touches and cherished belongings that reflect your individual taste and memories. Also, you described it in a temporary way without evoking the sense of permanence and belonging that characterizes a home. It sounds like you've been isolated for too long and lack connections and relationships with neighbors and friends that create a supportive community."

"I'm sorry to say this, but you are paying me for honesty and not empty reassurance. The hollow hole in the earth where you live is a testament to your unspoken loneliness. Furthermore, your self-deprecating humor about being housebound due to relentless blizzards and suffocating heat struck me as a mask for unbearable pain. Unfortunately, I must add that the fact you primarily communicate with online friends betrays a profound sadness. If you intended to be funny, your humor fell flat."

The room spun as I struggled to digest the counselor's scathing criticisms. How dare she look down on me with an oblivious ear to the truth. She couldn't possibly grasp the agony of losing my support network and every possession that held sentimental value. Her condescending, smug demeanor infuriated me. She had unfairly judged me from her high horse, with no idea of the fury boiling beneath my poker face.

I felt like a fierce volcano waiting to erupt as she instructed me to come to the next meeting "ready to describe your future in extreme detail." "Your 'homework' is to write a 1,000-word essay. I want to hear what décor and personal touches you will add to make your home a sentimental place where you feel relaxed. I'm also going to ask about your wardrobe. Today, you're dressed like a frumpy, pathetic loser. Step up your fashion game because that dingy pajama top speaks volumes about your headspace. Tell me about your most delightful and seductive outfits in your essay. I might also ask you to discuss the new relationships you'll be forming, given that you will be entertaining company soon."

Overwhelmed at the list of requirements, I just nodded, blank-faced, when she added, "And be prepared to discuss what you've written. Remember that looking at notes will be considered cheating."

Thinking of myself as a seductress who evoked desire and intrigue seemed like a mighty task. The idea almost floated over my head. But, at that moment, I was drowning in sadness and desperately reaching for a mental life jacket. After our first session, even though I felt numb and engulfed by a sense of hopelessness, I did my homework, as instructed.

The act of translating my dreams onto paper felt terrifying yet strangely exhilarating. I began crying as I realized each sentence reflected the painful reality that had left aching holes in my heart. As I cried harder and harder, tears became a lifeline that helped me to process gut-wrenching, unresolved grief.

Crying reminded me that I was alive.

Chapter 2

DO YOU WANT TO FEEL TREASURED, DESIRED, OR BOTH?

SYNOPSIS:

Positive visualization can draw you out of your insecurities and focus you on creating your dream future. I felt prepared for whatever the Motivation Counselor was going to throw at me at my next therapy session.

Instead of showing up wearing another dingy pajama top, I dressed in an elegant black turtleneck sweater and black skinny pants, washed my hair, and put on fire-engine red lipstick.

My counselor didn't waste any time diving into a high-speed assault.

"Question: What clothes will you wear when you go out on the town a year from now?" Confused about why she cared about my clothing, I replied, "I'm dressed simply in oversized, black prescription sunglasses and a graphic T-shirt. I wear a silky A-line skirt with platform, cork heels, and a black leather fanny pack across my right hip, gunslinger style. Oh, and I'm sporting a minimalist, practical wristwatch."

"'Practical' instead of 'extraordinary'? C'mon. Give me 100%," she curtly responded. "It sounds like you need help remembering your homework." Then, with more emphasis, she added, "I want to hear laser focus on what you see and describe. Imagine telling this story so that each word is a brushstroke. Give me character development! Show me what you see with vivid details. Be meticulous as you bring this painting to life!" She was almost shouting.

"Got it," I continued. "I see myself gliding into the room with the elegance of a Hollywood starlet. My slicked-back hair is styled in a low-hung, braided bun, and I'm wearing fire-engine red lipstick."

My answer was not a hit. "Is that all?" the counselor complained with a scowl. "Do better!"

"I weigh 20 pounds more than I do today, and I have glorious curves in all the exciting places," I said, refusing to be bullied.

The Motivation Counselor chuckled but moved forward quickly, asking, "What kinds of exercises are you doing besides hiking? And describe your favorite venues for entertainment."

"Hmm," I muttered. "I wrote down that I would learn to fly-fish and attend a balloon festival. And I'd do barre exercises to classical violin and cello music in my tiny, mirrored home workout studio."

"Discuss your future in the *present* tense," she demanded, like a drill sergeant. "Repeat everything, but this time, paint the picture for me in the present tense."

After a slight pause for self-reflection, and with my eyes tightly shut to avoid looking directly at her, I started talking again, slowly at first. "I tie amazing fly-fishing knots, and I sneak away to this top-secret, remote fishing hole on the shores of a shimmering lake. All I have to do is cast my line, and rainbow trout instantly hit the bait, one after another, faster than I can reel them into the boat." After a breathy sigh, I continued talking faster. "I'm at a Memorial Day balloon festival, watching hot air balloons launch into the sunset. There's dancing nearby, with live country music bands. Small children are holding stuffed animals and wearing glow-in-the-dark necklaces, standing in line at food trucks with their parents."

After another even longer pause, I started to get lost in my vision and continued dreaming aloud, picking up momentum. "I see myself at a rodeo show, holding my breath as I watch an agitated bull bucking, snorting, and kicking while his cowboy holds on for dear life."

After swallowing deeply, I kept painting my masterpiece with a flourish. "Local eateries are located on nearly every corner, so I enjoy people watching—sometimes inside a mountain café next to a plate glass window and sometimes while sipping espresso at a tiny table on the sidewalk, alongside the hustle and bustle of city life."

"Hmmm, keep going," she coached me. "And your diet? C'mon. Snap, snap!"

I hadn't expected questions about my diet, and she had barely asked about my décor after talking for so long about how my home sounded hopeless. I felt judged, misunderstood, nervous, and self-conscious. My mind went completely blank as I stared into space.

Clenching her jaw in disgust and furrowing her brow, the Motivation Counselor loudly clapped her hands above her head, demanding my attention. "Anybody home? Helloooooooo."

When she snapped me back to attention, I instinctively touched my trembling lip and felt the warmth of blood beneath my fingers. Shame washed over me. I hated myself for letting her verbal onslaught affect me so profoundly. As the metallic taste of blood hit my tongue, I realized that unconscious lip-biting was a tangible reminder of my vulnerability and proof that she was right. I really was "a pathetic loser."

My breathing was uneven as I held my tightly clenched fists in my lap. "Yes," I replied with a dull expression.

"Yes, what?" the Motivation Counselor demanded.

I'd worked diligently to complete this miserable, cynical, old wretch's homework, but the loud ticking of a wall clock nearby was distracting me. I anxiously struggled to remember the dreams I'd written down about my spectacular future life.

"I want to host small dinner parties for friends at my home. I'll be serving healthy foods and sticking to a diet full of plants and brain food like fish, with entrees such as salmon salad with dark leafy greens and an olive oil dressing. I'll drop crunchy walnuts on top for antioxidants."

Nodding in approval to myself, I explained, "I haven't found fresh pecans in the grocery stores lately. Then again, I was spoiled growing up near lush pecan orchards. The nuts I found at the store don't even look edible. I need my pecans fresh, or I can't eat them," I added, stuttering slightly.

"Enough rambling about pecans!" the counselor loudly interrupted, looking stern.

"In my essay, I wrote about feeling helpless and how pecans are my comfort food," I shot back, talking over her but stuttering again. "I rarely stutter these days, even though I remember that humiliating time in my life well."

"Let's not talk about the past, Dear," she responded. "It's common for me to counsel women who've lost their balance after long-term stress.

You're on track now. Stay in the present tense. Have you upgraded your exercise regime yet?"

I sat up straighter and tried to adjust my attitude. "Yes. It's been a while now since I walked with a cane. That's history. Hasta la vista," I confidently continued. "I'm doing stretching exercises at home, cross-training with free weights, and working out at a gym near the house."

"That's the spirit," the Motivation Counselor said approvingly. "You didn't let me trick you. Way to go for following the directions. You mostly stayed in the space of positivity no matter what I said that challenged you. Do you have any children?"

"I never had biological kids, but I was the primary caregiver for my parents when they fell ill. Mom used to point at me and say, 'She's the mom now.' She looked at me with wonderment as if I couldn't fail. I didn't allow myself to show anyone my vulnerability because so many things could have gone wildly wrong. I wanted her to believe she was safe, even though I couldn't always protect her."

"You're making progress faster than you imagine, Sweetie," the Motivation Counselor gently interjected. "Don't lose your focus. Your vibration is improving."

I was starting to relax when she suddenly threw another curveball at me. "On that note, what does your romantic life look like? I need a good love story with oodles of juicy details as my savagely uncivilized day started early."

I stared despondently at the floor.

"Start speaking NOW!" the counselor demanded.

"When you asked me to tell you about the new relationships I'll be forming, I didn't realize you were going to ask me about romantic partners," I replied hesitantly.

The Motivation Counselor wasn't down for hearing me complain. "Surprise me," she shot back, irritably.

I could have easily asked this grumpy old curmudgeon, "When would I have time to care? Don't you know my idea of a good time is to make it out of bed, shower, and keep breakfast down without battling nausea?" Instead, I tapped into a tiny spark of passion I was learning to channel from my courageous friend, Olivia. In an out-of-character moment, I launched into free-spirited, blissful improvisation.

"I see a gentleman king sitting close to me on a gently worn, brown leather loveseat, hidden between rows and rows of shelves at the little independent bookstore down the street."

Unimpressed by my outburst of creative flair, the Motivation Counselor responded flatly, "That all you got? I thought you were clever."

Feeling beaten, I held my head in my hands.

It didn't feel fair. She had not given me all the questions I needed to prepare for this meeting. The clock was ticking as I scrambled to think of what to say.

"Tell me about your *next* romantic relationship," she urged in a harsh tone.

Although I was utterly fed up with her unprofessional attitude, I did my best to answer the question. "I don't intend to have another long-term relationship unless it is with an intense and extraordinary new lover. He will have a strong, protective masculine presence, a huge heart, and impeccable character."

"Enough about his heart and his character. I want to hear about off-the-charts chemistry. Are you physically attracted to him? Make it easy for me to see how and why this individual plays a pivotal role in your destiny."

She instructed me to "take a minute of silence to picture his every detail in your mind" before I spoke.

I didn't enjoy being in the hot seat, but my answers became clearer as I begrudgingly accepted the Motivation Counselor's challenge. She clearly wanted me to prove I could shock her. It was also true that I had grown tired of seeing myself as a worthless, invisible mouse. After sitting quietly, I answered with calm intensity, "I'm falling for my sweet and devoted Arthur. I see his nose in a Guy de Maupassant book of short stories. He's wearing a black crewneck sweater with simple blue jeans, and the light in the bookstore is bouncing off his shiny salt-and-pepper hair."

Maybe the Motivation Counselor was only pretending to snore. It's also possible that she was a great actress. Either way, her disrespectful behavior was intolerable. She didn't seem to notice when I stopped talking for a moment. Olivia had said these sessions would be "brutal," but I hadn't expected to pay good money to watch my therapist sleep. Perhaps she regarded me as a lost cause. My cheeks felt hot, and I was seething inside.

The Motivation Counselor clearly knew she had pushed me too far when she finally looked up and saw my steely gaze. "Yes?" she asked through one squinty eye.

This cat-and-mouse game was tiring, but I needed to stand up for myself. "He winks at me and motions for me to follow him," I continued, lowering my voice. "I'm smiling because his cologne is fresh and irresistible."

My heart was pounding as I continued. "He smiles, and courage surges through me as he grabs my hand. I follow him through tall, winding stacks of books to the adult section in the back of the store, and I feel hypnotized into a sense of wild freedom as he pulls me toward him into a darkly lit corner."

At this point in my story, I noticed the Motivation Counselor was anxiously leaning toward me in her chair, so I abruptly stopped talking and watched the loudly ticking wall clock. I'd hooked my fish. It was time to own my power.

"And?" she coyly asked.

I held my silence as I continued watching the clock and counting in my head: one thousand one, one thousand two, one thousand three. At the 10-second mark, I glanced over both shoulders as if to scan my environment to ensure no one else was listening, even though I knew we were alone.

I continued the story in a slow, emphatic whisper. "We have a raw, visceral connection that transcends words; it's like a deep bond has been forged. I've never felt so intimately connected to someone and have reclaimed a part of myself I thought I'd lost forever. The rush of pleasure when I'm with him floods my body, making me feel alive in a way I haven't experienced in years. He fills my primal, insatiable hunger."

"Exactly *how* does he do that?" she inquired with more timid curiosity.

I took a moment, pretending to give thought to my answer. Now I had her.

"He makes me feel seen," I finally answered.

"I'm listening," she responded.

"I tend to be reserved, introspective, and private, and I take my time to open up. He allows me to get to know him at a comfortable pace. It isn't just the grand gestures that captivate me. He remembers the little things—how I take my coffee, the books I love, and the stories I share. On our second date, he surprises me with a picnic under the stars, complete with my favorite snacks and a playlist of songs with special meaning. It's as if he knows my heart before I do. He always opens the door for me and pulls out my chair, but it's more than just chivalry. He sends me handwritten letters expressing how much he enjoys our time together. In a world of texts and emails, that simple gesture makes my heart flutter. And you know what? He listens, really listens, to my hopes and dreams. And when he speaks, it's with such sincerity that I can't help but feel a connection that runs deeper than physical attraction. Every date is planned with thought—whether it's a cozy night at home cooking a meal together or an adventurous day exploring art galleries. He taps into my passions. When he surprises me with flowers, it's not just any bouquet; it's always my favorite bloom. He understands that I would rather receive one perfect gerbera daisy than three dozen roses. The bright petals of gerbera daisies make me lighthearted and remind me of innocent times."

"On our anniversary, he organizes a scavenger hunt that leads me to all the places that hold special memories for us. Each clue reminds me of how far we've come together. He surprises me with weekend getaways, planning every detail to ensure I feel pampered and relaxed. It's the thought he puts into these trips that makes them unforgettable."

"In the beginning, we had stars in our eyes, and our relationship was marked with giddiness and outrageous displays of affection. Now, we're in a more comfortable and grounded place. At the end of the day, it's not butterflies in my chest or bedroom fireworks that draw me toward him. It's the way he treats waitstaff and strangers with respect that speaks volumes about the kind of person he is. I love how he dedicates time to helping at local shelters, food banks, and community events. He will always offer his seat to an elderly person or pregnant woman, and he acknowledges his friends' successes, no matter how small. He helps with chores that aren't his responsibility, and he rubs my feet when we're watching our favorite series on television."

"I get that he's romantic. Let's go back to that cozy night when you're cooking a meal together. What's for dessert?"

The nerve of this woman, I thought to myself before loudly barking, "He has a nasty, rowdy, extremely creative, and thrilling imagination. He craves a delicious and electrifying *explosion* of *passion for dessert*!"

The Motivation Counselor's eyes grew wide in disbelief as she instinctively slapped her hand over her mouth in astonishment. I was fueled by a desire to *feel* something—anything that mattered.

"After dessert, I'm left with a euphoric afterglow that lingers, making the whole world brighter and more vibrant. I'm in love with him!" I shouted, loudly slamming my fists onto the arms of the couch in front of me and throwing my entire soul into this bold admission. Thoughts flooded my mind faster than I could speak as my gestures became more emphatic. If the Motivation Counselor had intended to stun me out of my zombie-like sadness by pushing me toward an electric vision, I was ready to show her how she had underestimated my fire.

As I continued to hold intense, direct eye contact, I lowered my voice again and declared, "He makes me feel desired *and* treasured."

"Now we're talking! You've found your determination, and I finally believe you!" my therapist exclaimed as she broke into a broad, spontaneous smile and clapped her hands in delight. "To be physically desired is a very different experience than feeling treasured. You want to fall in forever love, Sweetie. And you will.

"The first step to making that dream come true is to *expect to be lucky* in a new romance. Get ready for it because that day is coming soon! Remember that scientists do not fully comprehend the miraculous, sexy organ we call the human brain. Visualization affirmations can have a powerful effect. Trust that you can manifest your most incredible dreams."

She paused for effect, then she sternly announced, "Time's up."

The following week, we met for a follow-up online, and the Motivation Counselor asked me for an update on my relationship with Arthur. When I explained that "he's still back in that bookstore because you pushed me to talk about my intentions before I was ready," she closed her eyes and demanded that I "take this activity seriously."

Her austere, exact words were, "Make do."

Although I had the urge to roll my eyes and run, I began talking instead. The Motivation Counselor's gruff manner had jolted my brain into high-speed motion.

"So, we're sitting quietly beside each other, sharing a slice of homemade Sicilian pizza," I continued. I knew my crossed arms broadcast discontent, but I needed to finish this story, not for her, but for myself. Stating my thoughts out loud reinforced my desires, making them feel more tangible. Although I felt vulnerable, I spoke from my heart, saying, "We don't need words to communicate effectively. I would rather be right here with him than anywhere else."

I paused to more clearly envision two new local friends walking toward our table to say hello. "One is my Realtor® and the other is her adorable 70-year-old mom," I explained. "My friends can only sit with us for a few minutes because they're headed to a movie. Arthur tells them an embarrassingly corny joke, and we all politely laugh. People recognize his brilliant mind because of his expansive vocabulary. But what they remember most about him is how he makes them feel cheerful."

I paused again and closed my eyes as I envisioned the sweetness that I wanted in my life even more than erotic flames scalding the ceiling in moments of passionate, lost abandon. "Our time together is lighter than air," I continued. "I see the two of us walking hand-in-hand in the Garden of the Gods Park. We're looking at the stunning mountains and red rock formations, while sharing a cinnamon and white mocha ice-cream cone."

"It's marvelous to see you gain confidence. Where do you want to go next?" the counselor asked. She almost sounded like a nice human being.

"That's easy," I told her with an ear-to-ear grin. "I'm going to stand on top of the world!"

The Motivation Counselor appeared delighted with this response. "Outstanding! Attagirl," she stated as she loudly clapped her hands. "You've started to think big, and this skill will become easier as you practice. When you realize your real life is becoming what you now see as a fairy tale, you'll be inspired to work harder to merge your dreams with reality. Let's save the top of the world for our next visit. I also want to hear about your new business. Our time's up for today. Keep thinking about all the spectacular possibilities ahead. Stay focused on the amazing future you're creating."

I was smiling broadly as I walked away from our meeting. Every session with the Motivation Counselor had been a battle where I had fought not just against her words but against the chains of my past. As she forced me to relive my traumas, I became infuriated. Her harsh words made me question my worth and played on all my insecurities. She had cut through my defenses like a razor-sharp sword with chilling precision. Initially, she had talked to me in a voice dripping with disdain. But in our last meeting, she had cheered my progress in ecstatic delight. I heard her inspiring comments on a loop tape in my head over the next few weeks: "You've found your determination. I finally believe you!"

Ironically, the worst therapist of all time had become my unlikely muse.

Chapter 3

THE SCIENCE OF LISTENING FOR LOVE

SYNOPSIS:

Making a conscious effort to become more grateful for the different types of love in your life can make you feel younger, even as you age. By understanding the eight types of love first identified by the ancient Greeks, you may spot unhealthy relationships faster and more easily recognize when you're already enjoying true devotion from someone special.

As an undergraduate, I crushed on a journalism teacher who authored books about unsolved Southern murder mysteries. My unrequited love told our class to "seek to understand your sources by developing your ability to see their side of the story. Intensely focus your attention to listen and see the facts through their eyes."

According to handsome Professor Rapport, the principle of seeking to understand your sources in journalism by developing your ability to see the facts through their eyes was based on Aristotle's advice about the value of understanding others' perspectives. Aristotle advocated for empathetic listening and understanding as a foundation for achieving better communication and mutual respect. This principle encourages individuals to build collaboration and trust, which are key components of effective leadership and personal development.

Professor Rapport told us that improving our listening skills would enhance the quality of our writing. I assume he was involved in theater at some point, as he had a way with an audience. We were sitting on the edge of our seats, hanging on his every word. I remember him taking exaggerated steps forward and then snapping back to attention in front of our class. As he slowly scanned the classroom, he stopped to linger on each of us with laser-focused eye contact. We sat, frozen in place and entirely awestruck, as he stood there looking at us in silence.

His wide cheekbones, smooth, creamy skin, and jet-black hair drew you into his piercing, dark eyes, shaped like two perfect almonds. Giggles in the back of the room often broke awkwardly long pauses. I was not the only young college girl under his spell.

"Develop your ability to understand the person in front of you, and you could win the highest honor in American journalism," he confidently stated.

Professor Rapport made many large, choppy gestures when he talked with his hands. He was extremely fit and had perfect, bright white teeth.

"Do you understand the importance of hearing what someone *means* and not just what they *say?* Do you?" he asked. "I know a lot of lawyers who strategically say 'I hear you' instead of 'I understand you' or 'I agree.'

"Gentlemen, when you tell your girl that you think the two of you are on track to get married one day, and she replies, 'I hear you,' instead of, 'I agree,' you had better think long and hard before racing to put a ring on her finger. Buddy, this gal is on a different wavelength than you. Listen up. The words 'I hear you' mean something entirely different than 'I understand' or 'I agree.' Words are flaming, red-hot tips. They can be subtle clues to the motivation for a grisly crime. Likewise, they are giveaways that someone is lying and can even reveal that a woman has fallen madly and desperately head-over-heels in love. Listen more closely. Listen for love."

Professor Rapport talked about "tells" in poker—a clue to the cards the person in front of you is holding—explaining that a player can "tip their hand" by nuances in the words they choose when conversing. If a person says they have "decided" something, this individual just expressed that they put thought into a decision, whereas the words "I feel" and "I think" mean very different things. And if someone says "I feel" or "I think" often enough, they've given you tremendous insight into both their mental hardwiring and their motivations.

He told us it was probably Mark Twain who illustrated the importance of carefully choosing your words as "the difference between being struck down by lightning or a lightning bug." He also said that listening closely to someone's grammar when talking in their native language is another way to gain insight into their educational level and perspective. And he mentioned that a person's tone of voice and body language can matter more than their words. "You've got a couple of ears and eyes and only one mouth for a reason," he noted with a broad smile. "Do better than listening just to hear. Listen *and* watch their actions."

"Listening to understand what your subjects really feel and think is the secret to unlocking a prodigious writing career."

Professor Rapport turned his back to us before whipping back around to face us, inhaling deeply, and throwing his chest back. "Listening to understand is the key to what?" he loudly asked. The vice president of the honors society darted her perfectly manicured, dainty hand up in the air.

"Yes, Samantha?" he replied.

"Listening to understand is the key to winning the Pulitzer Prize in journalism," she enthusiastically answered.

Professor Rapport winked at Samantha and said, "Good guess, young lady." All of his female students lived for one of those winks. It was the reward for studying harder.

"Remember what I am about to say for the rest of your days," he told us before taking another deep breath and exhaling slowly. "Listening to understand is the fastest way to become more intelligent. Class dismissed."

Decades later, I remembered this early lesson about listening to understand. We can utilize this skill of listening intelligently to others to identify who has a real love for us and whose affection is a pretense. And don't forget that love comes in many forms. Let's return to the eight varieties of love that the Greeks identified. We all know that positivity is contagious. The Greeks recognized unconditional kindness for everyone, including strangers, as a type of love called Agape.

Philautia is the Greek category for self-love. Aristotle famously taught that our warm feelings for others mirror our feelings about ourselves, so this is intimately related to Agape. This notion underscores the importance of self-love. The idea that a smile can cause people to smile back in response was proposed in *The Expression of the Emotions in Man and Animals* by Charles Darwin, published in 1872. His observations on facial expressions, from joy to sadness, in his own children helped launch the field of child psychology.

The Greek label for blood-relative love is Storge, and the category for platonic love between friends and family is Philia. Interestingly, their culture valued friendship, love, and sacrifices made for comrades even more than they valued sexual passion.

To be pragmatic is to be practical. Pragma, like Philia, is not based on passion. Instead, Pragma is based on responsibility and a sense of loyalty and commitment. This glue has caused many married people who are no longer sweethearts to stay together long after losing their romantic attraction.

Ludus describes a love that is lighthearted, playful, affectionate, flirty, and fun.

Then there is Eros, the Greek god of fertility and passion. This type of love, full of primal sexual lust and fantasy, was considered irrational and dangerous. They felt this temptation should be treated with responsibility and caution.

Finally, Mania is obsessive love; it's where the word "maniac" comes from.

I'm surprised those deep-thinking ancient Greeks didn't include puppy love on their list. While it's true that a dog, however loyal, can't rub your feet or get you a glass of Merlot while they give you a back massage, an attentive fur baby can still provide vital companionship.

Chapter 4

CULTIVATE MORE APPRECIATION FOR YOUR SQUAD

SYNOPSIS:

In the same way that a green or blue environment can help you manage anxiety,[1] spending time with others can affect your emotions. Who are the individuals that energize you, and who depletes you? Is a friend your champion, or does he or she make condescending comments? Constant criticism may negatively affect your self-esteem more than you realize.[2]

---

1   Morgan, C. (2018) Mental Health and the Bar: How Choosing the Right Study Space Can Positively Impact Your Mental Health, Bar Exam Toolbox https://barexamtoolbox.com/mental-health-and-the-bar-how-choosing-the-right-study-space-can-positively-impact-your-mental-health/

2   Baron, R. A. (1988). Negative effects of destructive criticism: Impact on conflict, self-efficacy, and task performance. Journal of Applied Psychology, 73(2), 199–207.

Motivational speaker Jim Rohn is often given credit for the idea that you are the average of the five people with whom you spend the most time.

Want to learn Italian at lightning speed? Befriend a *bellisimo amico* who speaks Italian as a first language.

Or maybe you'd like to sharpen your memory and analytical skills? Try hanging out with a computer guru or a public librarian.

Then again, you might be aiming to improve your tennis game. If that's the case, it'll be easier to level up your abilities if you regularly play with someone who can beat you every "game, set, and match."

There's an old saying about some people being in your life for a season while others appear for a reason. Most of us have told confidences to a new friend or fallen head over heels for a lover without taking the necessary time for diligent vetting of character. The GGs' advice is to practice watching someone's actions for long enough to truly get to know them. This goes for *all* your relationships. Walk away from meddlers, snoops, gaslighters, and takers so that you'll have time to meet supportive individuals with whom you have more in common.

As I said above, Jim Rohn's theory is that you will become like the five people with whom you spend the most time because they have so much influence over you. This uses the law of averages, which, for example, might help define the market value of a building for sale by taking the average price of the five most similar properties.

With a nod to this rationale, one of the fastest ways to reinvent yourself as a happier person could be to reconnect with dear old friends. Have you lost touch with someone who inspired you to take healthy risks? In high school psychology class, we learned that "belonging" ranked third in Maslow's hierarchy of needs. It's human nature to want to feel acknowledged for your contributions.

- Who remembers your birthday without a social media prompt? Have a card ready for their special day.
- Is there a longtime friend who wants to have lunch but only gets in touch on short notice when they're passing through town? Try to make time to catch up when that call comes in.
- And who is it that cares when you have surgery? When they go through something similar, put a note on your calendar to visit or send flowers during their recovery.

Think of that girlfriend you would call to pick up medicine and chicken soup for you when you can't get out of bed due to illness; volunteer to run errands in *her* time of need.

I interviewed a woman named Carla, who told exciting stories about the direct relationship between the value of her time and her self-esteem as she described her closest friends. Like Carla, I want my social network to be comprised of healthy, solid friendships, and I want to show appreciation to the people who treat me with the most respect and kindness. Carla and I discussed the importance of carefully choosing in-person and virtual friends.

"Both of my parents are gone," she explained. "I work hard to make sure my friends feel valued and know how much I love them because I'm single, and they're the ones I count on as family now. I'm a fixer because it's my nature to try and solve problems for the people I care for. One of my best strategies for sustaining balance in my personal life has been creating distance between myself and toxic individuals. Maintaining my peace of mind requires cutting out negative energy."

Carla explained that she felt guilty and stressed about loosening ties with an old friend named Anastasia, whom she described as a wild child in a lab coat. According to Carla, she and this 50-something physicist had been friends since college. She said Anastasia had a voracious appetite for men that drove antique hot rod cars and distilled pure, unfiltered moonshine.

Carla also noted that Anastasia had an analytical, scientific mentality and could open your mind to a universe of sexy possibilities. She said her friend could tell time using the sun and confidently navigate a sailboat. She furthermore admired how Anastasia was always on the lookout for meteorite showers, which she described as facilitating the absolute best time to "go parking." However, Anastasia cautioned Carla about "dangerous romantic activity" in the ocean under a full moon because she thought sharks may be more likely to attack. Carla stated that if she had inquired further about what dangerous romantic activity meant, Anastasia probably would have elaborated about adventures with studded dog collars, handcuffs, feathers, and other "passion props."

She explained that her friend encouraged her to consider wildly creative, out-of-the-box options for keeping life as a single person simple, such as separating the urge for "snack festivities" from the desire for a monogamous, physical, and emotional relationship. Anastasia was, according to Carla, "a free-spirited anomaly who reminded her that climax is only the result of muscle contractions, a raised heartbeat, and heightened blood flow." Carla also noted, "I would not be giving Anastasia credit if I didn't mention that she could be one of the most empathetic human beings I've ever known when she's in the mood to give a damn about me." Carla said that, although she missed her "self-absorbed" pal, "We both have the same 1,440 minutes per day to spend however we choose, and I couldn't waste more of my minutes solving emergencies for a user."

"Building new relationships while you let go of golden older friendships isn't easy," Carla continued, with her hand on her hip in the power woman pose. "I know I was addicted to caring about Anastasia and that it became a lopsided, out-of-balance relationship. You asked me to tell you about my best advice for living well, and this is it: Cutting negative energy from your life is mandatory when you're living in a state of never-ending fight or flight. My message is that self-protection is self-love."

Psychiatry pioneer Karl Menninger theorized in his 1958 book *Love Against Hate* that the people we spend time with can have more impact on our lives than our genetic predispositions. Carla's interview left me with questions about navigating friendships. My biggest takeaways were the need to choose my sounding boards more carefully and the importance of developing new connections. I wanted to develop a keen awareness of who energizes me and spend more time around optimistic people.

One of the women I regularly call when I need an emotional lift is my artist friend Angie, a fashion photographer. Angie meets pretty people all day and incorporates their best practices into her beauty routines. She's a knockout, but she is also humble to her core. I've never known someone who has survived more bullets in life and emerged victorious. I see her as a force of nature. It's always been enjoyable to get her insight into international politics. Thanks to Angie's input, I've become more aware of how other countries view the United States. Simply put, knowing her makes life better.

Another headliner in my closest associates who deserves more attention is a childhood friend from across the world, where there's a 12-hour time difference. Juliana ran a corporation until recently, and she has a husband and two children. I've observed that she carries more responsibility than most of my other friends, but she whines less than anyone I know about the difficulties in her life, which include facing cancer. I've never met anyone who expresses gratitude for all her blessings more often than this brave soul. Thanks to her attitude, I've learned to say thank you more frequently in my prayers and to pray more often. When Juliana's company was shut down for several months during the pandemic, she still had large bills to pay. It must have been humbling for her to cook and sell simple boxed meals to make ends meet and support her family and staff. Despite these challenges, I recall her sweetly telling me that she and her husband are grateful they could lean on other skills to care for their relatives and "staff members, who are like family." I also remember her describing love as synonymous with responsibility. As Juliana said, "We were carefree back in school, but now we have more love to appreciate. The proof is our high level of obligations."

I've called my adorable confidante for advice on countless occasions. Plenty of times, however, she's volunteered unsolicited opinions that I didn't like. You know someone loves you when they tell you what they think you need to hear, even when they accurately predict the information will be hurtful.

Juliana was also my elderly sick aunt's friend. She understood how much my Aunt Alicia prized the experience of getting out of the house and regularly took her to her favorite seafood restaurant, which overlooked the riverfront. This normalized my aunt's life and gave her events to look forward to in the future.

I went missing right after Aunt Alicia's death. But I received about a dozen back-to-back messages with uplifting music videos from my dear friend Grace. It must have taken Grace hours to find online links for all those songs. Her playlist of healing tunes was an incredibly thoughtful gift to help me cope with grief. Grace is a spiritual advisor who spends her free time doing hospital volunteer work for people near the end of life. If a talented illustrator were to draw her, they would sketch two stick legs coming out of a big, smiley-faced heart. I treasure every moment of our conversations because, as previously mentioned, friendship is a limited-time gift. I don't take her optimistic influence for granted. Although she is highly sought after for counseling services, I'm lucky enough to be a friend and not a patient.

Comedian Chris Rock, who is known for advising others to "listen to people that are smarter than you," often talks about trust issues and vulnerability in relationships. One of his jokes explains my loyalty to Grace perfectly. "You know you have a true friend when they know all your secrets and still choose to be your friend!"

Chapter 5

EASY WAYS TO MELT GRUMPY HEARTS

SYNOPSIS:

This chapter will address the GGs' thoughts on how to foster goodwill with people, affordable ideas to show loved ones they're valued, and better ways to discuss your flaws and insecurities.

If you're having difficulty with people, you can often foster goodwill by sincerely complimenting them. If that gruff handyman you hired to stop your refrigerator from leaking seems distracted, for example, there's a better way to ensure the work gets done correctly than wringing your hands and hovering nearby with a worried look. Maybe he stayed up all night caring for sick children, or he might be silently suffering from a migraine. While it's true that some individuals think "good enough" is a high bar, many can be motivated to improve with the right encouragement and a donut. Try saying thank you to someone like that handyman by telling him, "You did an amazing job. Here's a tip to help you pay for your superhero cape."

As explained in the introduction, the strategies presented here aren't one-size-fits-all. Carla from Chapter 4 shared a story about her free-spirited physicist friend, Anastasia, who melted overzealous police officers' hearts. Carla recounted how Anastasia has charmed her way out of speeding tickets by batting her eyelashes and asking playful questions like, "Is it too late to say I was just trying to outrun my problems?" or, "Would it be possible for you to write 'future driver of the year' instead of a ticket?"

Of course, everyone has weaknesses. We're all human, after all. Whether you're interviewing for a job or meeting a friend to take a jog around the block together, it matters how you ask for leniency regarding your mistakes. I recently saw a supermarket manager use incredible patience and diplomacy to ask for mercy from a customer. The grocery store line was long just before dinner, and a frustrated shopper vocalized his annoyance about the lack of checkout clerks. "I know," the manager calmly replied. "Being short on staff tonight is my fault because I'm a hopeless softie. I gave Gladys the day off as a reward for being voted Employee of the Month for the third time this year. She's a single mom with five children who hasn't taken a day off in over two years. And Sam's not here today because he needed to attend his son's funeral."

After that explanation, a man toward the back of the line loudly asked, "Where can I apply for a job?!" Everyone in line laughed, including the critical customer. It was a sweet reminder of our shared humanity and how a moment of frustration can be transformed into a moment of warmth.

Stuck for creative ideas for outings to refresh connections with longtime friends?

- Find an orchard, and enjoy picking fresh fruit together.
- Take goofy photos of one another in front of local street art murals.
- Rent scooters and find the perfect downtown spot for a picnic.
- Volunteer for a local tree-planting event.
- Grab a couple of kites and coolers and head to the beach.
- Bring coffee in canteens for an early morning sunrise hike.
- Embark on the noble quest to sample craft beers at a local brewery.
- Read the same book and discuss it over dessert at the corner bakery.
- If you're feeling brave, sign up at a local open mic night.
- Spend an afternoon channeling your inner ornithologist with binoculars, insect repellant, a field guide, and an app to identify bird calls. Who doesn't want to be the coolest bird watcher in the park?

Maybe you want to brighten the day of a friend who just had surgery. Wish them well with a sweet, simple gesture such as:

- Luxuriously creamy homemade butternut squash soup, with hints of nutmeg and cinnamon, and a cryptic crossword puzzle involving wordplay and anagrams. (Who knew the word "listen" could be rearranged to form "silent"?)
- A fleece blanket and a selection of herbal teas, including spicy ginger, invigorating peppermint, and a chamomile blend with floral notes and a hint of apple.
- A gourmet cookbook with high-end recipes found in upscale restaurants and a cute bookmark.
- Lemonade lip balm and a small, potted peace lily to purify the air or
- A luscious lavender bubble bath and fuzzy slipper socks.

- One of my all-time favorite presents is a delicate, handmade antique handkerchief adorned with beautiful hand-crocheted edges. It's the kind of treasure you stumble upon in charming little antique shops while wandering off the beaten path during a road trip. These vintage treasures are infused with sweet memories and a sense of nostalgia.

Chapter 6

DRESS FOR SEXY OPTIMISM

SYNOPSIS:

Chromotherapy, widely known as color therapy, can be traced back to the Egyptians. Enjoying a functional wardrobe of brightly colored bras and panties can be a relatively inexpensive strategy to help you feel less anxious and acknowledge each day as a fresh start. This is just one of many simple tactics to refine the way you dress and curate your closet.

Refining your secret signature style can be an act of empowerment that makes you feel sensual and elevates your self-image. And the right base layer of lingerie enhances the fit of outerwear. Picture a collection of dazzlingly bright bras and panties as an elegant, budget-friendly method to manage anxiety. When you want extra courage for a big presentation, pick that bright red bodysuit. Reach for pink panties when you'd like to feel more girly and feminine and save the orange undies for days when you're sluggish and lacking energy. And what about when you need to calm down quickly? The feel of your magenta nightgown's luxurious, silky fabric against your skin can prepare you for relaxing, sweet dreams.

You are a precious angel with a playful edge. You're meant to be adored and spoiled. Don't let a lack of Benjamins get you down. Whether you occasionally feel lonely, yearn for a more attentive partner, or are enjoying the freedom of being single, intentionally choosing the perfect colors for your teddies, camisoles, and bralettes can elevate your vibe from the inside out. Great times to shop online are when big box retailers offer huge discounts:

- Black Friday
- Cyber Monday
- The Fourth of July
- New Year's Eve and New Year's Day
- Martin Luther King Junior Day
- Easter
- Memorial Day
- Labor Day
- Mother's Day
- Father's Day
- The last Saturday before Christmas

When introducing a new piece of lingerie into your capsule collection, bid farewell to at least two items you haven't worn in the past year. This approach will help keep your intimate wardrobe fresh and make it easier to stay mindful of your spending. Think about investing in versatile pieces that can be paired with existing items for endless styling possibilities.

Embracing a minimalist approach to your closet will foster a greater sense of abundance and gratitude in your life. You purchase fewer pieces that last longer and make you happier. As you curate your small closet of staples into stylish outfits, you realize that organization has become fun. It also makes traveling easier. Just toss a pair of high-quality jeans, a buttery-soft black leather motorcycle jacket, and a couple of graphic tees into a suitcase for a weekend wardrobe. Beyond wearing clothing that boosts your confidence, you surround yourself with supportive people and seek out environments that enable you to be your best self.

As you pause to glide your fingers over the soft fabric of your lucky, crimson red, velvet button-down, you recall sweet associated memories of fabulous places and remarkable people. This beloved top has been one of your favorites for more than a decade, and because you care for it well, it remains in perfect condition.

Now you check your chest of drawers to see if anything has slipped your attention (corny pun intended). You light a scented candle, wash your hair, and apply bright red lipstick to give yourself some Hollywood glam and the illusion of whiter teeth. You'll soon be using those white teeth to smile more often. Clever queens like you avoid analysis paralysis and obsessing about an uncertain tomorrow by investing themselves entirely in the now.

You're paying full attention, and that includes awareness of your surroundings. Your sunshine-colored sweater helps you walk with more spring in your step, but you're street-smart enough to know that flashy attire could also make you a target for crime. When venturing into crowded public venues, you usually try to keep a low profile because you know better than to stand out. And if mixing with the masses, you'll make the safer choice of neutral outerwear. A plain, black overcoat can cover all your fabulousness with a little mysterious and effortlessly chic *je ne sais quoi*.

You will be in good company. Time-strapped fashion designers and legendary creative entrepreneurs are known to lean on black wardrobes to save time and mental energy. Maybe you'll wear sexy undies beneath an all-dark outfit that travels well. Or, if it's snowing, you might get creative with layering. Finding new ways to express your signature style can become a source of pride. Luckily, money-saving outfit generator apps can make discovering new options nearly effortless. Almost every item in your closet should work with other pieces and each piece should be a wardrobe workhorse. Remember the childlike joy you felt dressed in your fanciest Sunday best? You'll be amazed at how many chic combinations your playful adult self can discover.

My dear Aunt Merry Joys has never met a stranger, as the saying goes. When she visited me in Colorado, we went sightseeing, and I was astonished at how many people commented on her sassy, colorful outfits. MJ coached me to purchase clothing as an investment, using a cost-per-wear (CPW) strategy. The CPW strategy is about buying high-quality, classic items that tend to hold up better over time instead of wasting your hard-earned cash on trendy, mass-produced choices that quickly fall apart or go out of fashion. The idea is to invest in wardrobe staples you can wear frequently and for a long time, thereby getting more value from each item in your closet.

Trying to squeeze into clothing that's too tight can make you look silly. If you've gained a few pounds and are struggling to fit a bigger bottom into your skinny jeans, try a few deep knee bends for a stretched-to-perfection fit. Sleep in them. Work out in them. Wet them down and try to pull them out to a larger size. Then repeat as necessary. This goes for T-shirts as well. If you want the best-fitting graphic tees on the planet, buy them a size too small, then gently stretch the fabric over your chest and shoulders for a more expensive-looking fit. Obviously, you'll occasionally overstretch an item until it's unwearable with this technique, so I often purchase gently worn, budget-priced clothing at resale stores, and I prefer to try this trick on older apparel which I rarely wear. Testing a fabric's limit is easier when you have less to lose.

If I could only share one anti-aging rule, it might be: Wear a hat in the sun—the bigger, the better. I have a sun allergy, so I'm attached to long sleeves, sunscreen, and large, statement brims. Years ago, I attended a convention with at least 500 others, and I remember hearing attendees talk about "that guy in the enormous hat." People stood in line to meet this man because everyone was curious to know who he was. As it turned out, he wasn't a celebrity or even a conference speaker. At some point during a long day of speeches, in a breakout workshop, I sat next to Enormous Hat Man and commented on his unique style. He smiled and gave me advice I'll always remember: "Ma'am, it's not who *you know*. It's who *knows you*. This hat makes friends for me."

On Saturday nights in Colorado Springs, long lines of people stand outside the country and western bars in flashy cowboy hats and exotic boots featuring mesmerizing tooling, stitching, and hand-embossed patterns. The best-dressed cowgirls avoid campiness by wearing simple, flowing dresses or jeans with elaborately embellished footwear. Unless you're a rodeo star or a country singer in costume that could double as a parade float, it could be considered gauche to wear multiple western-themed clothing items simultaneously. But who doesn't love a good "What in tarnation?" moment?

Life will be more enjoyable if you have fun with what's on your feet because lighthearted hues and tantalizing textures can wake up the senses and keep you alert. For me, finding the ideal fit in a pair of caramel and ruby red boots was an adrenaline rush because I had to become an expert on comfortable footwear after bunion surgery. Gorgeous, highly pointed, closed-toe-torturers are no longer an option. To this day, the surgery area throbs painfully, so it's always a relief to find attractive shoes with a boxy toe area.

Got a pair of leather pumps that are slightly too small? Try sliding pint-sized freezer bags filled with water into the toe area and leaving them in the freezer overnight to stretch them out. Genuine leather strappy sandals can be your friend as well. Look for sandals with straps that perfectly fit areas that are prone to pain. To understand the variety of more accommodating—but still pretty—sandals out there, search online for "celebrities with ugly feet." You'll appreciate your own tootsies more after seeing photos of your favorite movie stars' grotesque foot corns and wonky hammer toes.

Comfortable footwear is essential to standing and walking with grace and beaming confidence. When you allow your shoulders to slump, your spirits will likely be half-mast, and you'll broadcast misery. But by standing tall, like a tower of feminine power, you'll project positive energy. For an easy advantage in life, research how models carry themselves. Then, modify your catwalk strut for real life. Why *walk* into a room when you can *glide*?

Besides projecting yourself as more polished, standing tall can help lessen tension in your back and neck area. Your newly improved posture will also be beneficial in controlling headaches. I know women who sit for long hours working at the computer, and several of them complain about migraines. We've also discussed how high heels can cause the muscles behind your legs to tighten up to your spine. It's fun to confidently strut in sparkly spikes, except when your feet scream in pain. In my mid-30s, working as a fit model and convention speaker required long days of standing. Other models at the Apparel Mart in Atlanta, Georgia, taught me to alternate shoe heel heights when walking or standing for long periods to give my feet a break.

I've been inspired by feisty senior role models, like Aunt Merry Joys, who take fashion risks. There shouldn't be an expiration date on style when we stop dressing our best and updating our hair and makeup. A highly functional capsule wardrobe can help you cultivate an easy, breezy demeanor and provide motivation to develop more love in your life.

Chapter 7

LASER FOCUS ON THE PATH TO SUCCESS AND WATCH IT MATERIALIZE

SYNOPSIS:

It was easy to merge women's identities in this book because the main characters shared similar war stories and showed the same determination. Whether or not it was clear to the Guardian Gals™ I interviewed, I began to believe that the happiest women I've met led simple lives and didn't always distinguish between goals and reality. Like high-achieving athletes who consciously "rewire" their brains to experience wins before they occur, they envision the specific steps to achieve their biggest dreams with clarity and intense motivation.

Research in neuroscience suggests that daily visualization prayers can trigger neurons in your brain to activate success. More than one famous golfer has asked "God" or "The Universe" for help, then pictured every major and minor detail before making the perfect swing. Similarly, most of the Guardian Gals™ I spoke with mentally practice becoming powerful magnets for attracting sensuality, high-quality love, and financial and physical health.

The stories in this chapter were inspired by a husband-and-wife team who founded a real estate school. "We jam six months' worth of information into a three-month class, with weekly tests," the wife stated. "To get an overall passing grade, you must intensely listen and commit several hours a day outside of class to studying. About a third of our students will drop out within a few weeks. The ones who make it through to pass the final exam can become top salespersons in the local market. If you flip the switch on your reticular activator, you can excel here and join that elite group."

Crystal explained that the reticular activator system is "a part of your brain that, when triggered, causes you to pay more attention to something once you've noticed it for the first time with focused interest." She stated, "Understanding how this works can help you get an A grade or meet your future husband."

This couple had playful banter and sizzling chemistry. It was easy to listen to Crystal's story about how her husband motivated her to activate the reticular activator system in her own brain. "We hadn't been dating long when he asked me to wear pink for a Valentine's Day date," she noted. "When he met me at the door, he picked me up in a rented pink sports car and handed me a gorgeous bouquet of a dozen pink roses. The thought he put into our first date was incredibly romantic. I felt swept away, as if in a scene from a movie. He made me laugh and feel adored."

"When there's a goal I really want, I go after it," he announced. His eyes sparkled with mischief as he showered the class with air high-fives and twirled his wife around in a whirlwind of silly dance moves. We howled with laughter as she pretended to faint in delight. Crystal beamed and blew him an air kiss when he described their marriage as "the most important deal I've ever closed."

She noted that, "He made reservations for dinner at a fine dining restaurant housed in a restored 1888 Victorian home that was painted pink. Men had to wear jackets for dinner." Crystal laughed, asking the class, "Can you guess what color his was?"

"I was shy back then, but I left pink lipstick kisses all over his cheeks that night," she added. "How could I have avoided falling in love with this gorgeous, crazy boy?" she asked us as she wiped tears of laughter off her cheeks.

"I had never seen a pink sports car before in my life!" she continued as her dance partner took an exaggerated bow. "After that first date, I started noticing other pink cars around town, and my eyes lingered on little girls riding pink bicycles and wearing pink bows in their hair. Even the pink candies at the convenience store looked tempting. He put a spell on me! I couldn't avoid thinking about a future with this darling man because he made himself unforgettable." Crystal noted that, after meeting her husband, she "began to associate pink with the feminine joy that filled my thoughts when I opened my mind to the possibility of falling in love."

Crystal paused to blow her husband a kiss before announcing that she had eventually become so clear and focused on their success as a team that their long, happy union was a foregone conclusion. "And *that* is how you need to see the information in this class. If you take nothing else from tonight's class, remember to create a crystal-clear vision of your success-filled future, and don't let go of that dream!" she concluded.

"If you only want to get into real estate to make money, you enrolled in the wrong school. There's the door," she firmly stated, pointing at the exit. "If you don't plan on learning how to become a master of real estate, leave now, and we'll refund your admission fee. If, however, you want to have the time of your life and succeed beyond your wildest dreams in a thrilling career, then wake up your reticular activator and begin to visualize your spectacular future."

These are just some of the tips that Crystal gave to her class about how to start on this journey by paying attention to the things that will propel you forward:

- Stop and smell the sunflowers at your local farmers' market. See yourself handing clients a bouquet of these happy flowers after your first successful closing.
- At your first closing, picture an orange and black monarch butterfly migrating thousands of miles to glide through an open window and gently land on your nose.
- Add honey-colored sticky notes to what you learn in class to help you memorize the material.
- Wear saffron socks and use yellow highlighters to remind yourself that our most successful graduates study at least three hours at home for every 60 minutes in class.
- Your reminders can be sunsets and sunrises.
- Pick meaningful colors and symbols for your future dreams and keep them in front of you.
- Post answers to the questions you expect to see on the mid-term on your refrigerator.
- Leave your textbook open on your kitchen counter to remind yourself to study.

- Record yourself reading your notes aloud and falling asleep to the recording. Turn the recording back on when you wake up. Play the recording when you're driving to class.
- Ask to interview the most successful real estate agents you can find and identify themes in their advice; then add notes from those interviews to your recording.
- Pay attention to how the top agents dress and what cars they drive. Watch television shows that feature real estate agent superstars.
- Start noticing all the "sold" signs around town. *See* yourself becoming successful as you meditate on every detail of what success looks like.
- When you get an A on your final, call your friends and tell them about your victory. Share your enthusiasm for showing their properties.

Chapter 8

CREATE AN ENCHANTING PLACE TO CALL HOME

SYNOPSIS:

After exploring chic home décor boutiques and scrolling through striking social media feeds to ignite your imagination, you'll find it easier to envision your living space as an organized and sophisticated sanctuary. Let your creativity flow as you create an enchanting place to call "home."

Observing how someone you care about chooses to live can provide invaluable insights into their character. Is their space cluttered and dark, or is it relaxed, light-filled, and inviting? Does bright energy and love permeate their environment, reflecting their inner state? The way they arrange their belongings, the colors they choose, and the presence of personal touches all tell a story about their values and priorities. A tidy, well-organized space may indicate a sense of control and peace, while a chaotic setting could suggest underlying stress or confusion.

Pay attention to the small details—a scientific digest on the coffee table, its spine worn from countless readings, thriving plants in every corner, or vibrant artwork adorning the walls. Each element contributes to a larger picture, revealing layers of personality and taste. The book suggests a love for trending topics in environmental science, while the flourishing plants hint at nurturing tendencies. The artwork, whether a bold abstract or a serene landscape, speaks to the owner's creativity and provides important clues to their interests and passions.

Just as vibrant lingerie can brighten your day, a calming color palette and relaxing décor can help you unwind and recharge—because who doesn't want to feel like an empress while binge-watching their favorite shows in velvet sweatpants? Refresh your space by finding new uses for your favorite and most elegant items.

- Turn luxurious faux fur coats inside out and drape them over chairs or hang them in a corner to add texture to a room.
- Stack elegant vintage suitcases to create a chic side table that adds character and storage.
- Get more use out of unique teacups and handcrafted pottery by using them to hold fresh flowers or small succulents, adding an artistic touch to any room.
- Hang beautiful serving platters as functional wall décor in the kitchen.
- Display polished gold flatware in a glass vase for a striking table centerpiece.
- Hang a beautiful rug to make a bold statement and add a sound barrier to a shared wall.
- As for your collection of hardback books? Showcase these beauties in short stacks that guide the eye along a colorful path through your home, much like street signs directing traffic. If you

stack them high enough, they'll also double as a stylish safety barrier against your cat's latest mischief.

In my living room, the most functional decoration is a life-size ceramic rabbit, Mr. Fitzgerald, who is dressed in a dapper vest and coattails. With his playful smile and larger-than-life personality, he serves the unexpected purpose of holding my reading glasses. When I'm not wearing them, they rest on his nose. He stays perched on a stack of books on a spare dining stool, and guests frequently ask where he came from, dubbing him "the coolest eyeglass holder ever." I have proudly explained, many times, that I found Mr. Fitzgerald at a thrift store, but he's worth far more than the five bucks I spent to rehome him.

I also love discovering different ways to utilize everyday household items. For example, baking soda can refresh and sanitize your refrigerator, freshen your breath, remove product buildup from your hair, and make jewelry sparkle. A friend said that baking soda even saved her life during a Thanksgiving oven fire. Thinking on her feet, Sally grabbed a box of baking soda from the fridge and used it to extinguish the flames. She later told me that it releases carbon dioxide, which puts out fires, whereas water can worsen a grease fire.

While we're on the subject, I recently learned that you should never open the door to a building if there's only one and the room is full of flames. Indeed, the reverse is true: Always close the door to a room that's on fire. I had a kitchen fire a few years ago. A relative was present, and she raced out the door to get help, closing it behind her. A fireman told me those flames would have spread much more quickly if that door had been left open.

According to the Motivation Counselor, eliminating clutter in your house can significantly enhance your peace of mind, and tidying up is associated with improved memory. Also, remember that cleaning can feel less burdensome when you wear earbuds to listen hands-free and tap the mute button on your smartphone to mute your voice and block out distractions.

Have you ever noticed that being prepared reduces the likelihood of emergencies? Many women I know lead overscheduled lives, making time an even more precious commodity. A lavender hair 38-year-old professional speaker on memory enhancement, named Lana, shared that maintaining work life-balance was easy for her because her home is designed for efficiency.

She said she hangs her keys on a rack by the door, sets her morning alarm on auto, and wears a simple work wardrobe so she doesn't need to make clothing decisions. Lana stated, "I even stick to a few healthy breakfast meals on rotation. One of my favorite time-saving hacks is making overnight oatmeal before bed. Using glass mugs lets me see the pretty layers of fresh fruit and nuts. Pretty food tastes better."

Lana told me she follows the art of Feng Shui to bring harmony into her home. She does this partly by collecting elephant figurines for good luck and filling bowls with citron crystals to attract financial success. When I asked about one of the bowls of crystals sitting on top of a stack of adorable notebooks, she proudly explained that she was coaching a client to write down creative ideas to improve her memory.[3]

---

3   According to Betty Edwards, an American art teacher, author, and lecturer with a Master of Arts from California State University, Northridge, and a Doctorate in Psychology, Art, and Education from UCLA, you can activate electrical activity in brain regions responsible for memory when you write your creative ideas down by hand.

Chapter 9

THE LAZY COOK'S GOURMET SECRET

SYNOPSIS:

Upgrading your diet doesn't have to be complicated. This chapter reveals a tantalizing trick for gourmet cooking that can transform your meals into elegant feasts. This secret can make your dishes more mouthwatering, affordable, and healthier, all without breaking the bank.

Are you ready to turn your kitchen into a fragrant paradise? If whipping up healthy, beautiful meals feels overwhelming, it's time to embrace this delightful cooking hack for lazy chefs. If you have a wholesome diet focused on whole grains, greens, nuts, berries, and less processed food, you're already on the right track. Now, it's time to turn your healthy habits up a notch and tantalize dinner guests. For just a few dollars each, grab some pre-grown, indoor potted herbs, and you've got a wonderful mini garden. Besides being affordable, it can feel like an easy magic trick to maintain your collection of gourmet garnishes.

Whether you're looking to boost your metabolism or catch better zs, there's an herb, spice, or seasoning that may work wonders for your health.[4] Consider purchasing an inexpensive DNA test to understand the risk of any life-threatening genetic conditions in your family, then explore the medicinal properties of cooking herbs that can help solve potential health issues. Don't worry about getting lost in research; seasoned gardeners generally agree on about a dozen herbs that are incredibly popular. Rosemary, basil, thyme, mint, parsley, oregano, chives, and bay leaves are easy to grow in an indoor garden.[5] If you don't mind kitty walking across your kitchen counter, you can even add catnip to that list.

I highly recommend sweet basil for your first experiment with growing herbs for cooking. It's an annual that can quickly offer big rewards for a small amount of effort. Just snip its leaves, and they'll spring back faster than you can say "fresh pesto."

With food prices soaring higher than ever, it's time to tackle grocery shopping like a pro. Arm yourself with a list and hit the aisles on Mondays or Tuesdays to dodge the crowds. Embrace the mantra, "Prepare food once, then eat all week," and watch your time and money stretch further. Cook in bulk, and stash those delicious leftovers for later. Why not pre-cut a zesty mix of vegetables in a large container on Sunday night? Think colorful carrots, crunchy bell peppers, and fluffy egg whites to jazz up your sauté. Remember, sharing food is a heartfelt way to show

---

4   According to this Mayo Clinic article, published in May 2022, you should choose foods that promote skin, hair, and nail health: https://www.mayoclinichealthsystem.org/hometown-health/speaking-of-health/get-radiant-hair-skin-and-nails-naturally

5   Stacey Leasca and Lisa Milbrand listed herbs that are generally the most popular and easy to grow in an article they wrote for *Real Simple,* published on March 21, 2023.

love—especially when you garnish your meals with fresh herbs from your garden, turning every dish into a memorable feast.

Don't settle for the same old ingredients in your fridge when you can create culinary magic with the yummy flavors of your indoor herb garden. Picture yourself tossing cooked spaghetti in golden olive oil, then sprinkling in garlic, a handful of fresh, homegrown parsley, and a dash of salt and pepper. Just like that, you've elevated your meal to gourmet status with *un delizioso spaghetti aglio e olio*! Plus, that parsley doesn't just add flavor—it may also play a role in cancer prevention.[6]

Keep your poker face in place while asking company, "Would you like a little pinch of fresh rosemary with your spaghetti, or can I cut several stalks for you?" Guests will likely take you up on your offer to add "several stalks" if you explain that rosemary may help you grow longer, shinier hair.[7]

A family friend we call "Cowboy" often ends phone calls by saying, "Have fun!" He's a wise man who often reminds me, "Young lady, the quality of your memories is the quality of your life." Cowboy's philosophy is simple yet profound, and it's a reminder that the joy of preparing and sharing food can create lasting and unforgettable memories with others. Indeed, cooking comfort meals can both invoke all your senses and give you a reason to invite friends into your beautiful home. Let cooking inspire you to take that leap and make plans with those you love.

---

6 According to an article posted on Ohio State University Comprehensive Cancer Center's The James blog on July 21, 2023, parsley contains the flavonoid apigenin, which may have cancer-fighting properties. https://cancer.osu.edu/blog/five-herbs-that-could-reduce-risk

7 According to this study published in *Advanced Biomedical Research,* rosemary can improve the health of your hair: "Evaluation of Herbal Hair Lotion Loaded with Rosemary for Possible Hair Growth in C57BL/6 Mice," March 21, 2023. https://pmc.ncbi.nlm.nih.gov/articles/PMC10186041/

Chapter 10

BE THAT HOSTESS WITH THE MAGNIFICENT MOSTEST

SYNOPSIS:

"Hygge" refers to the Danish concept of feeling comfy and convivial in your home. You can't have too many supportive people in your life, and planning a creative get-together for the folks who care about you can be easy. This chapter is narrated through the eyes of Patty, a retired party planner. Although she formerly organized large special events full of hygge for her clients, she prefers to host spontaneous soirees of two to three friends these days. Patty playfully quotes celebrities, including Andy Warhol, who once stated, "One person is a lonely number. Two people are a couple. Three is a party."

There's nothing more special than being invited to someone's home for a visit, and treating friends to surprises can be good for your mental health. Entertaining guests is an act of sharing that can compel you to dig out your pretty clothes and vacuum your living room floor.

My favorite party favors are tree cookie coasters, which I get from my local arborist. He gives them away for free instead of throwing hundreds away every day. These have been such a hit. When a girlfriend raves about my coasters, the next time I see her, I'll give her several "cookies" wrapped with a red bow and a mint sprig for a refreshing surprise.

I like to plan small dinner parties on a Friday night, as I've learned that's generally the easiest time for friends to visit after work. Guests are likelier to show up if you confirm a time in person or by phone. Experience in sales cold calling, when I was a party planner, has taught me that Tuesday at 9:30 in the morning is the best time of the week to ask anyone for a few minutes to talk. If I'm trying to get the attention of a close friend, I generally text a brief message first, such as, "Can you talk for three minutes?" Then I keep my word and watch the clock, so I don't keep them on the phone any longer than that. People are more relaxed on Tuesdays because they've had the chance to get their bearings for the week, and they've usually been able to make a cup of coffee by 9.30 am. I always send a follow-up handwritten invitation and text reminder the day before an event.

When I used to help clients host larger get-togethers, I told them that, as a general rule, 80% of the invited guests would say yes and follow through. With that expectation, there will probably be cancellations, so it's wise to ask a few more people to attend.

There are plenty of excuses to celebrate with friends. Some of the party themes I've used in the past include:

- Taco 'bout a party!
- Pasta la vista, baby!
- Wine not?!
- Murder mystery and meatballs
- And Chili cook-offs to spice up your life

I've talked with numerous social media influencers who mentioned their love-hate relationship with meeting people online because a long-term focus on virtual friendships can cause unrealistic expectations and fear of missing out. I personally try to limit social media interaction and take time-outs for digital detoxes that significantly improve my mental well-being. We all have a limited number of days to enjoy the lovely people in our lives. I enjoy setting the table with my finest dishes, playing soft jazz in the background, and treating my guests to the flavors of my cooking. Everyone has their own special talent, and mine is crafting melt-in-your-mouth meals. Ha! As Muhammad Ali once said, "It's not bragging if you can back it up," and I'm here to prove it!"

If the weather's beautiful, I might call a few friends and ask them to join me for a backyard tea party wearing a silly hat. I like to shower each new guest with confetti, then introduce them to the gang.

Great snacks are critical. Mini cupcakes topped with sprinkles, lemon scones, and maybe even some outrageous *hors d'oeuvres* that look like they belong in a culinary art exhibit will make your event unforgettable. As for games, I can recommend challenging your friends to a croquet match or a horseshoe showdown. The possibilities for laughter are endless when you grab your fanciest, silliest hat and prepare for an unforgettable afternoon filled with joy, friendship, and just the right amount of chaos.

Holiday parties can be a kick, too. I was lucky to have a simple, sweet childhood growing up by the riverfront. My family observed Christmas with a tree decorated with dried sand dollars as ornaments. After the holidays, just before dismantling our tree, we broke open the sand dollars, which released five "doves" that stood for the joy of Christmas.

These delicate shapes, reminiscent of small, white birds, are actually the sand dollar's teeth that have come loose. There's something truly special about gathering with friends and family to break open dried sand dollars together. It's a shared experience that's far richer than video chatting. Other meaningful, non-denominational holiday-gathering ideas include:

- An ugly sweater party;
- Creating a cozy viewing area with blankets, pillows, and popcorn and hosting a girls' night holiday movie marathon;
- Inviting guests to share their favorite dish at a potluck dinner party;
- Hosting a mid-morning brunch with a spread of pancakes, pastries, and mimosas; and,
- Planning a holiday themed scavenger hunt around your home or yard.

The options for a fun house party are endless. It can become even easier to create camaraderie when you invite a few friends to come early and help as co-hosts.

Chapter 11

REDEFINE YOURSELF AS FREE-SPIRITED AND FIT

SYNOPSIS:

This chapter presents strategies to become healthier and more adventurous, from exploring music and art therapy to a "sexy skit night." Before test-driving some of these tactics, be aware that once you become more independent and carefree, others may criticize your choices.

Listening to classical music with solid beats could cause you to think more clearly. It's common knowledge that many parents believe in "the Mozart effect" and play his compositions to their babies to help them relax and become more intelligent. It wasn't surprising to learn that some hospitals offer music and art therapy.

Back in Savannah, Georgia, I took art therapy classes with an angel who teaches enhanced emotional expression and improved self-awareness by helping her students create fine jewelry. Chrissy's studio is a safe space for students to process their feelings and explore mindfulness and personal growth.

When I wear the sterling silver talisman I made under her supervision, I also wear a smile. Creating my treasured FREEDOM pendant enabled me to feel a sense of calm at a time when nearly everything else in life was going wrong. With Chrissy's inspiration, I rediscovered how getting lost in a creative flow can be like an oxygen infusion that revitalizes your spirit and gives you a sense of accomplishment.

On the early morning walks to Chrissy's zen-like studio for sunrise classes, it was easy to dream about strolling through an enchanted forest on an exotic safari. There's value in early morning meditative outdoor walks. Studies have shown that one hour of fresh air and early sunlight boosts your serotonin and can increase your life expectancy by two hours.[8]

Her utopian live-work space had an open view of the backyard through full-length windows. The garden was bursting with yellow and red wildflowers and colorful hand-painted gourds swinging in the wind. Other students' shiny, unfinished gold and silver rings and bracelets were artfully strung across workstations. She is a master jeweler, yet she has never, to my knowledge, heavily promoted her own work. I suspect her greatest joy comes from teaching others to achieve their dreams. My former art therapist bursts with pride when she talks about her students' artistic creations.

There were a few sessions when I asked her to skip teaching scheduled class material to counsel me. When I confided about how I struggled

---

8   https://www.webmd.com/a-to-z-guides/health-benefits-morning-walk

to protect family members as my own physical health spiraled, she asked me to remember that when you make huge sacrifices for goals that don't work out like you'd planned, you often walk away stronger. Chrissy encouraged me to journal in the tattered little notebook I carry around. We discussed how putting your thoughts in writing can make clarifying your most important truths easier. In retrospect, I've learned that the more ideas I recorded, the faster I reached important personal revelations that empowered me to reclaim my grit.

Journaling quick thoughts became an outlet for creating lighthearted, mood-changing energy. To this day, I scribble silly poetry, especially during difficult times. The following example is called "My Apologies to Real Poets":

Oh, you think I'm silly?
A skinny South Georgia hillbilly?
I'm indeed no rhyme hero,
And my poetry skill is zero.
But look into my heart,
And you, too, will see,
The magic power of positivity.

Colby is a good friend who patiently endures my lame rhymes and always surprises me. I often wonder what she's going to say next. When I asked her what she does to unwind, she said, "I like to smell good. And I wear minimal clothing and a feminine, sweet little ankle bracelet during the opening act for our 'fire hot, sexy skit date nights' to push away the jitters." Colby then shared that her new boyfriend reads to her "emphatically and with tremendous feeling" as the pre-show for "Make Out Saturdays." She declared that she feels safer and calmer when in love and explained that she fell hard for him after his heartfelt renditions of classic, romantic poetry by E.E. Cummings, Pablo Neruda, Anne Sexton, William Carlos Williams, Edna St. Vincent Millay, and D.H. Lawrence.

- Expect your reading glasses to fog up as you enjoy "Somewhere I Have Never Traveled" by E.E. Cummings, who expresses the unfamiliar awakening of emotional vulnerability with powerful, lighthearted sentence structures.
- Pablo Neruda's poem "Sonnet XVII" evokes the heat of a lover's touch by using rich metaphors to express the intensity of feeling both treasured and desired.
- In "The Farmer's Wife," Anne Sexton explores the sensual tension between yearning and reality with a confessional style. Her erotic imagery captures the raw energy of bittersweet passion and romantic desire.
- William Carlos Williams' poetry often celebrates exquisite experiences of the body of the body, such as in "The Red Wheelbarrow." In this work, Williams subtly invokes sensuality through the imagery of ordinary life. The poem's simplicity suggests that desire can be as palpable as the freshness of a rain-soaked garden.
- Edna St. Vincent Millay's poetry is rich with erotic themes, particularly in "What My Lips Have Kissed" and "Where and Why." This lyrical exploration of love's fleeting moments captures intimacy's captures intimacy's enthralling emotional dimensions. Millay remembers past lovers with nostalgia.
- And if you enjoyed D.H. Lawrence's frank portrayal of sexual liberation in Lady Chatterley's Lover, prepare for the discomfort of turbulent, cherished memories in his poem "The Rainbow."

If you're single, make Saturday about self-care and enjoy yourself! If you have a lover, ask him (or her) to take a deep breath before slowly reading these erotic adventures to you aloud. Tell them to linger on poignant lines and allow their tone to deepen as they share the passionate dance of language with you. Explain that you want them to let the weight of each phrase settle, leaving you breathless and yearning for more before they move on. Each word should roll off the tongue like honey, dripping with warmth and intimacy.

~ ~ ~

I'm grateful for the protective guardians who advised me to laugh instead of getting lost in analysis paralysis. Connecting with them is a refreshing break. I don't go one day without missing my most loving cheerleader: Mama. Her wellness advisors taught her to maintain an upbeat perspective as she explored the ancient practice of mindfulness, which can lower blood pressure and improve the immune response.

In addition to attending her doctors' visits, I was present for conference calls with her psychiatrists, psychologists, gastroenterologists, neurologists, ophthalmologists, nutritionists, occupational and physical therapists, and other specialists and counselors who consulted with me as her primary caregiver. I listened in the background as various authorities told my mother that optimism was the best medicine to fight illness.

With my own health failing due to stress overload, I visited a Savannah-based doctor who had gone to school in Europe and then continued his education in the US, going on to earn the highest professional respect in America. Dr. Progressive specialized in helping professional athletes overcome injuries. When he asked me to learn a two-minute meditation procedure, I listened to his instructions respectfully. This technique involves finding a quiet place to sit comfortably and focusing entirely on your breathing for at least two minutes. If you want to experience intense relaxation, be still and absorb the following example as slowly as possible. Then, keep your eyes closed as you go back in time to revisit one of your own favorite memories.

While doing this mental exercise, I revisit my memory of living in California and going window shopping at a favorite, luxurious outdoor retail and entertainment complex. I always feel my heart beating faster while descending the entranceway escalator, which takes just over a minute. In my meditation, I start from the seventh-floor parking garage and glide past lower floors to the entrance of the outdoor mall area, where the escalator stops at a luxurious gold-gilded sign that says "Welcome." From there, I walk through the crowded courtyard to the Las Vegas-style water fountain and see the trolley pass me by, filled with cheerful visitors. Then I cross the street and head to the bookstore café. I try to notice every detail along the way.

Riding up the three-level escalator inside the bookstore, I see an enormous overhead banner promoting upcoming events. I feel calm and upbeat as I reach the top level, passing the nature and travel sections and noticing colorful journals for sale. I head into the coffee shop and order a large pistachio frappe. Then, I walk out to the small outdoor balcony, which has luxurious seating overlooking the grand plaza. Many of my Los Angeles friends have yet to learn about this private gem for cozy sit-down meetings. I take a few appreciative deep breaths as my troubles melt away while I enjoy feeling the light breeze on my face at one of my favorite nooks. Then I shut my eyes tightly, appreciate the simple pleasure of the experience, and make one final wish. When I open my eyes again, I often realize that many of my dreams are already coming true.

A terrific follow-up to that kind of meditation is a brisk walk while window-shopping. This free retail shopping therapy can help you prepare to navigate around roots and rocks when hiking mountain trails. Whether you're a speed window-shopper or hiking in the woods, a walking regime can improve your overall strength and stamina, making you less susceptible to injuries.

My banker motivated me to find the best local trails after she told me she had begun running as a mental health strategy following her nervous breakdown. I was stunned that a relative stranger would graciously volunteer such personal information. But she said that knowing she was an inspiration to others had been her most powerful tool for recovery. Barbara told me she dropped out of medical school in the final stretch of her residency when she started fainting from the pressure. Failing on the last leg of her educational journey caused her tremendous embarrassment, but she reclaimed her self-esteem by learning the basics of running and going on to win marathons.

When Barbara asked why I moved to Colorado and what my experience had been like, I told her the headlines about taking care of my mom. She then asked her assistant to hold all her calls while she took her lunch break. When she shut the glass door to her office, leaned back in her leather chair, and began reminiscing about her comeback, I felt sure that this story would be epic.

Barbara claimed that a walking, hiking, and running program including "superlight arm weights" had worked as a preventative measure to slow her osteoporosis. She also stressed the dramatic impact that hydration can have on your body and noted that even mild dehydration can profoundly affect your health, make your thinking unclear, and cause digestive issues. As we age, she noted, it can become more challenging to recognize thirst, and so we need to drink more water whether we feel thirsty or not. Barbara told me she eats chia seeds before marathons because they help her run faster and farther. She claimed these tiny seeds help her to stay hydrated because they can absorb up to 12 times their weight in water.

A little while into our conversation, Barbara reached under her desk to pull out a huge plastic water bottle with time markers on the side—from

7 am to 9 pm—as reminders to drink. She said she sometimes adds slices of lemon to her water to aid in digestion and help fill in fine lines and wrinkles. However, she also cautioned me that lemons can cause inflammation and trigger skin conditions. This woman couldn't have been a day over 35 years old. The truth is, I didn't see any wrinkles—or even fine lines—on her face, but since she had admitted to an agonizing struggle with perfectionism, I didn't argue.

Barbara also said that when she indulges in too many cocktails, she drinks coconut water for the electrolytes that help her absorb moisture. Interestingly, my friend Kristin gave me the same advice. She said her wedding makeup artist taught her about drinking coconut water as a shortcut to dewy, plumped-up skin. Kristin stated that drinking significantly more water helped reduce her hair loss. She told me that another secret to her shiny hair was brushing for two minutes in the morning and then again just before bed, using a 100% boar bristle hairbrush to restore shine and texture.

I told Barbara that it's been interesting to notice how many Colorado restaurants bring a water carafe to your table. I've lived on both coasts, and I was always given a glass of water in the East but never a whole carafe. Barbara said that on the weekends when she's at home, she puts a fresh pitcher of water on her kitchen table first thing in the morning and leaves it out all day until she finishes drinking every last drop. She told me, "You have to be careful how you use electrolytes," but said that when she's going on a run and expects to sweat heavily, she'll add powdered electrolytes to her bottle to improve water absorption. She also mentioned that her running buddy, an oceanographer, fills novelty ice trays with blueberries to create "blue octopus ice cubes" to jazz up his water.

Barbara added that she occasionally gives herself a ripe banana or a juicy peach as "a cheat treat." However, she said that she's trained herself to cut up and freeze fruit just before it gets overripe and that she eats slightly green bananas for "early morning carb energy" because overripe fruit metabolizes as sugar.

When I got home from our meeting, I followed up on this memorable discussion by researching the effects of dehydration. Barbara might have been too uncomfortable to mention that not drinking enough water can also cause urinary tract infections.[9] Given my new location in a dry Colorado climate, I followed her advice and began to drink water with electrolytes. While reading labels on sports drinks, I found that my favorite-tasting brands had extremely high sodium and potassium levels.

Consequently, I decided to mix half a packet of sugar-free electrolyte powder into a jumbo-sized water bottle for daily hydration after exercise. A high-quality, stainless-steel bottle that made the water taste better was another no-brainer purchase. I also found a cute ice cube tray with pink heart cutouts that I fill with lime, lemon, and blueberries for a flash of color in my all-day water carafe. Since meeting Barbara, I've become a fanatic about freezing fruit before it overripens. Pineapple chunks, carrots, and celery can be cut and stored for a tasty smoothie, which is even more delicious if you start with an over-the-counter, low-sugar, and low-salt drink base made from healthy vegetables. Adding almonds or walnuts and blending those ingredients with lemon juice and ice makes for a fast, hydrating snack or meal replacement.

Everybody knows that your skin gets dehydrated quickly when you drink alcohol. An old joke in Savannah, Georgia, goes like this: In Atlanta, Georgia, they ask you what you do for a living. In Macon, Georgia, they ask you where you go to church. In Augusta, Georgia, they ask you about your grandmother's maiden name. Then, around Savannah, they ask you what you want to drink. If you know anything about my hometown, you've probably heard about our famous St. Patrick's Day Parade, which

---

9   https://www.mayoclinic.org/diseases-conditions/dehydration/symptoms-causes/syc-20354086

starts in front of the building where I formerly lived. Many downtown residents leave the city during that celebration because they don't want to be around rowdy drunks when the streets are blocked off. But, in my biased opinion, there's never been a bigger, more joyful party. That said, an important rule about small-town life is that word travels fast, meaning if you don't know your business, your neighbor does.

It broke my heart to recently learn that a high school classmate had died of complications from alcoholism. I remember being alarmed the last time I saw her because she had a ruddy complexion and was extremely thin. Heaven gained an angel when Lilly Beth passed away.

On a lighter note, my cholesterol significantly improved after eating oatmeal every day for six months. Dr. Gaudry said she'd never seen anyone drop their levels that dramatically. I may or may not have mentioned to her or her assistant, Benita, that I had previously been living off cheese and vegetable omelets. I also probably didn't tell them how much our dog enjoyed his daily game of One String Cheese for Me, One for Puppy. It was time to be healthier, even though I still fight the urge to binge on massive quantities of cheddar.

Once you start to eat a more balanced diet and grow your confidence, you can expect to experience more gratitude. It's also probable that your newfound contentment may evoke feelings of jealousy in others and even an urge to criticize you. Individuals you care about may compare their struggles to your apparent ease and believe your happiness is undeserved or effortless. Don't forget that criticism can speak more to their personal battles than to your achievements.

I hope your struggles become easier with every pause you take to savor the little things that bring you joy. You are capable of overcoming anything that comes your way. I thank Mama for her reminder to "wear kindness as your armor and always carry your water bottle."

Chapter 12

TURN YOUR PUSSYCAT INTO A TIGER

SYNOPSIS:

I had countless happy memories from my decade as a caregiver. Still, near the close of that chapter, I was newly divorced and felt disconnected from my body. A book about reclaiming your self-esteem would not be complete without mentioning the need to maintain your plumpest, pinkest lady lips. If they're not sweetly fluffy, and if you're not currently in a physical relationship, why not seek out a robust alternative to release anxiety?

Now, I'm no doctor, but I'm fortunate to call internationally celebrated intimacy counselor Dr. Gaudry a cherished friend and former high school classmate.

After Dr. Pam threatened to stop working with me unless I fully embraced her professional advice, she advised me to focus on self-love and put a vibrator in my hand.

Dr. Pam is a highly-respected legend in the world of OB/GYN. She has successfully coached thousands of men and women to get reacquainted with their sexy sides. One of her superpowers is teaching ladies around the world that you need to use your wildcat regularly if you want it to purr. And what will happen if you ignore her advice? Picture your pussycat turning into a dried-up, pinkish-gray old prune. If thinking about your lonely lady garden makes you squirm, you're not alone.

It's incredible how you can come to see someone you've known for most of your life so differently in the blink of an eye. Dr. Pam is a devoted Christian who invites her patients to join her Bible study. Call me old-fashioned, but I was flabbergasted by the long, neon pink play toy she gifted me after a lecture on self-love.

Her first book, *Love, Sweat & Tears: The Menopause Romance Revolution*, was made into a movie with major stars, including Jenny McCarthy, Dr. Michael B. Beckwith, and Joan Rivers. *Love, Sweat & Tears* explained that the happiest women are having the most sex.

Dr. Pam has encouraged thousands of women to wake up to her message—often after handing out neon pink treats at conferences and events. Her message? Most gals can enjoy a more vibrant sex life into their 90s if they have the energy and desire. Her mission is to help others enhance their intimate relationships, especially after life-altering events like menopause or surgeries.

No matter where you land on the body positivity scale, the need to get oxygen circulating in your private parts is critical if you want to avoid vaginal atrophy. Sadly, according to Dr. Pam, many women lose interest in intercourse, even when their equipment can still be rejuvenated because they stop caring about their bodies and get lazy.

Today's luscious bedroom gadgets allow you to indulge yourself and test-drive fantasies without a partner. Several of the women I spoke with about sexual health confided that new technology has leveled the erotic playing field. It's said to be easier than ever to explore positions on your own as you enjoy your most delicious fantasies.

A girlfriend of mine in Georgia had never heard about age-related vaginal atrophy. I had five seconds in the sun of feeling like a woman of wisdom when she asked me to tell her what I knew about turning back time in the Deep South. When I mentioned that my doctor had said she sometimes prescribes probiotic supplements and hormone therapy treatments, including topical vaginal estrogen, to keep things moist and manageable, I quoted Dr. Pam: "How long would you go without putting lotion on your face?" I also explained that, according to my brilliant MD friend, when you lose a dramatic amount of weight, your labia majora can start to look stretched and old, and your face can become gaunt for the same reason.

Friends, if you've been overwhelmed by life and want to recover your vitality, time is of the essence. Have you been to an adult toy store within the last five years? If not, let me just say that high spirited storytellers for this book said you don't know what you're missing. According to them, fingers are fun, but new cordless, rechargeable massagers are exciting inventions that have been dramatically improved since the days of loud, awkward, battery-operated bunny rabbits.

There wasn't anyone else in the adult toy store when Helen came over to help me out. She made me feel immediately at ease as she peered over the counter at me through oversized, vintage cat-eye glasses. To call her colorful would be an understatement. She had a heavy Cajun drawl and smacked peppermint gum in perfect sync with a nervous eye twitch. Helen said she met her husband online and that they initially only got together for "anonymous, lusty liaisons." She noted that she had been fighting severe, near-suicidal depression because her ex-husband had refused to touch her for more than a year. "It was a severely unhealthy situation," she explained. "I can't believe I stayed married in a sexless relationship for so long, like an orchid without water."

Helen said she saw herself as "an educator" and that it was her job to help her primarily female customer base "learn how to make their bodies sing." I got the feeling nothing shocked this fast-talking, gum-chewing New Orleans gal. She even told me that helping her mother-in-law pick out "a first-class toy collection" had given her a tremendous sense of accomplishment. According to Helen, physical intimacy helps your immune system, lowering stress and blood pressure, improving heart health, memory, and bladder control, burning calories, and helping you sleep.

Helen stated, "No woman should have to go through an excruciatingly long period without being touched and feeling loved because the most erotic intimacy happens in the heart." She insisted that couples could have a blast in bed without using more than their lips and imaginations. There are many ways to carnally connect with a mate at a soulful level. And there are just as many paths to pleasure without a partner. She tells her single customers that if they want more time, energy, and self-esteem, they should develop their toy drawer and get busy living their best life without worrying about meeting a romantic mate.

Helen wasn't the only woman I knew who married her friends-with-benefits liaison. When I met Fioralee in a yoga class, she had been in a long relationship with a high school football coach, to whom she is now married. Fioralee swore that, for more than a decade, they were "only about licking, pounding, and touching without talking." Then, one day, years into the relationship, they accidentally discussed achievements that mattered to them and became emotionally intimate. It's been more than a dozen years since this couple's wedding, which they had near the football field where they first met. I've never known two people who seem happier together.

Lana, the lavender-haired public speaker from Chapter 8, had a different take on avoiding private area atrophy. With a wink, she defined "savory-sweet appetizers" as "heavy making-out sessions, with exploration featuring fingers and tongues. She said she didn't want to have intimate relations outside of a monogamous relationship because she preferred to fall in love with one adorable "love wand" at a time. Lana also mentioned that every time she's been physically intimate, she's given away a piece of her soul. This admission led to our discussion about the importance of not handing out a piece of your soul like a stick of gum and why it's called making "love" for a reason. After all, if we were talking about making "clean dishes," the result would be sparkling silverware instead of pregnancy, an oxytocin release, or falling in love.

Lana had a knack for using food analogies to describe her romantic relationships, which made for entertaining conversation. Whenever we met, she seemed to have a snack in hand, and she'd draw parallels between her munchies and her intimate encounters. Her coat pockets were always stuffed full of tiny boxes of raisins, and she carried small plastic bags in her purse with nibbles like peanut-butter-covered apple slices or caramel-covered almonds. Lana claimed to have an aversion to fast food and fast men.

Another subject that came up in our conversations about adult pleasure was uses for the extra-large, triangular-shaped cushion. If you've ever worried about developing varicose veins or want to energize your gorgeous lady gams, you may want to closely evaluate pillow therapy. Top-secret girl-talk surrounding these underrated treats is often focused on how they can help train your muscles to clench tightly and hit all the best angles. Elevating your legs for short periods has potent benefits. It can be a healthy physical and mental release to breathe out exhaustion when you put your tired toes up in the air and improve blood flow to the lower part of your body. Likewise, going to bed with your head on a hard foam wedge may assist with acid reflux, enabling you to breathe more easily when recovering from a cold or the flu.

A sexy cat told me it can be easier to get in the mood for pillow talk by trimming your pretty flower into a heart-shaped landing strip or even a luscious lightning bolt. Professional waxing will remove dead skin cells, but more than one lovely lady mentioned the potential for painful complications. Another suggestion for adding a little edge during erotic interactions was a non-piercing feminine clip.

I promise I wasn't eavesdropping when a reality TV star gave memorable advice to her friend while standing on the other side of the ladies' locker room. This larger-than-life personality loudly told her confidante, "Girrrrl, let him cut it. I'm telling you that trimmin' that big ol' bush of yours can set fire to his foreplay. Don't take this opportunity away from the boy. Let him take his time in the area to create his masterpiece."

These women were curvy, well-endowed divas with dragon-long, multi-colored fingernails. They wore cotton crop tops with deep cutouts, matching lime-green, spandex workout shorts, and silver weightlifting shoes. Maybe they were both on the show. I'll never know because I don't watch reality television, and I didn't dare interrupt their conversation. I did, however, recognize the woman from the grocery store tabloid covers as brave. After all, who the heck wants to let a man loose with a razor down there?

Regarding other olfactory pleasures, lavender Epsom salts have been known to provide a luxurious soak. But luxury bath bombs and scented products may mess with your PH balance.[10] As for solo bathtub fun, you might try watching a steamy film that's hot enough to melt your computer. Don't feel ashamed. Smiling sources in the know have said that many women order "fabulously forbidden women's novels online and watch smoldering shows through streaming services." It's been said that experimenting with both and viewing a few trailers can be a mood-changing experience. However, one GG noted: "You'll want to avoid tapping on internet sites that can trigger malware and advertisements with pop-ups featuring male anatomy, which will shut your computer down."

If you need another delicious option when you miss "the significant other experience," you can always eat dessert first. The phenylethylamine in dark chocolate is believed to trigger hormones that can give you a chemical rush that's been called a hold-me-over substitution for love. Enjoy a few pieces daily for a quick mood boost as well as antioxidants to make your skin smoother. To keep your daily dosage consistent, drop frozen chunks of chocolate into steaming hot oatmeal for a nice breakfast treat. And say yeeeeees to dark chocolate melted on high protein, homemade, whole grain waffles.

Interestingly, research suggests that dark chocolate has polyphenols, which may also help improve insulin sensitivity.[11] After assisting my mother in taking her diabetic shots every day for years, I'm eager to follow every precaution to avoid following in her footsteps. But here's the naked truth: Cheating on your diet is occasionally good for the

10 Alnuweiri, T. (April 18, 2017) Are Bath Bombs Wreaking Havoc on Your Vagina? Fashionista.com https://fashionista.com/2017/04/bath-bombs-vagina-health-problems

11 NIH, National Institute of General Medical Sciences (February 14, 2020) The Chemistry of Chocolate, News Wise https://www.newswise.com/articles/the-chemistry-of-chocolate

soul if you can do it without dire health consequences. Sometimes, the answer to a bottomless pit of loneliness can be the taste of homemade Southern fried chicken with a glass of good champagne. While alcohol and greasy foods are not exactly a diabetic's bestie, the champagne will cut through the grease as well as your heartache faster than you can say, "Give me some fried deliciousness." Don't laugh until you try this low-country delicacy. It's cheaper than therapy and much tastier.

Chapter 13

YOUR BESTIE IN RUFF TIMES

SYNOPSIS:

Consider adopting a dog if you feel lonely and need the perfect listener, personal security, and an energetic hiking buddy.

Life is rarely dull for long with the right fur baby. Picture yourself researching different breeds' personalities and talking to dog owners about their experiences. Maybe you already own an extremely social pet who enjoys play dates and would appreciate the company. Do you need more home security? There are a lot of variables to consider, including how much free time you'll be able to dedicate to caring for your new friend and how another animal in your home will get along with the new resident. Dog food, toys, clothing, and vet bills will be expensive, but you can't put a price tag on loyal companionship. Ask your vet for his or her opinions. If you can make it work, a new pup might be an inspired idea when the time is right.

Just before Mama died, I asked her to write down her favorite memories in a pretty journal. Her first story was about how "Puppa" had made her laugh. The following excerpt is a delightful example of how a pet can keep you entertained while reminding you that personal space is a myth when you own a dog.

"When I was nine, Daddy brought home a very young, precious mixed-breed puppy that thrilled me. Puppa grew up to be a large, robust dog with a beautiful, long, reddish coat. Back then, we had an almost deserted beach only about 10 miles from our home. We turned Puppa loose to run in the surf, and he would bark loudly at anything unusual, such as a washed-up jellyfish. Of course, we knew we had to take a beach towel to clean the sand off him before traveling home. Since Aunt Cora was visiting us and wanted to go to the beach too, we let Puppa sit upright between my aunt and me in the back seat. We hadn't been at the beach long before I caught Puppa eating a stinky, dead fish. My family laughed for years about our trip home on that hot day. Our formidable Puppa insisted on stomping his sopping wet front feet over my lap and hogging the window beside my head. My aunt had the full impact of Puppa's wagging, bushy tail and his potent flatulence, although it permeated the entire car. All we could do was laugh, hold our noses, and wind the windows down."

Mom noted in her diary that her father was Puppa's favorite person. She said Grandpa would throw "nuggets of food" for Puppa as a reward for tricks, like a sliver of a sour pickle. Mama also wrote that Puppa "learned to be a quick long-distance spitter" and that my grandpa roared with laughter while Puppa waited patiently to continue the game. She said Grandma knew a healthier snack for Puppa would have been plain cucumber or fresh dill and that watching her dog eat salty food made her feel guilty. But laughter made their world go round. Mama took him everywhere, and his gregarious nature helped her conquer being painfully shy. She said he loved to race down the street while pulling her on roller skates that she attached to his leash with a rope.

My dog, Funny Bone, had a big personality too. I used to take him to dinner at his favorite local restaurant, where patrons eat from shiny, stainless steel dog bowls while their pups play together in a dog pen. That sweet, white ball of fluff loved his bright red sweater that helped me keep track of him when he bounced through the snow. I miss Funny Bone's bursts of energy and the way he would run around in circles at high speed, which we called "zoomie zooms." It broke my heart to lose my bossy little buddy to kidney failure, but I cherish our sweet memories.

Chapter 14

MAKE FINDING YOUR FUNNY SIDE A SERIOUS GOAL

SYNOPSIS:

Doctors say laughter is the ultimate medicine because we physiologically change when we laugh. A resounding "ha, ha, ha" will force stale air out and allow fresh air back into your lungs, lowering your adrenaline and stress levels.

While you may not be able to change the world, you can find hilarious silver linings, even in stressful situations. Research suggests that people who make others laugh and who laugh more at themselves are more likely to be perceived as having higher IQs.[12]

It's no secret that humor is a solid coping strategy. Nationally celebrated Atlanta comedian Jeff Justice has mentored thousands of aspiring

---

12 Dorthwaite, L. (October 19, 2017) Funny People Are Also More Intelligent, According to New Research World Economic Forum, Industries in Depth https://www.weforum.org/agenda/2017/10/funny-people-are-also-more-intelligent-according-to-new-research/

jokesters in his workshops, teaching students how to turn painful experiences into comedic gold. Justice teaches that good comedy is 10% material and 90% delivery and that leading your audience down a road with a surprise twist at the end can be a great way to get laughs. He convinces his students—and audiences across America—that humor can help a person survive hard times. It's like a life jacket made of whoopee cushions.

Laughter can be contagious, and spending time around people who turn problems into punchlines is an easy way to lighten your own load. Juliana, from Chapter 4, who described love as synonymous with responsibility, once shared her amusing struggles with American vocabulary. Though English isn't her first language, this sharp-witted gal figured out that corny puns could be a great source of comedy, especially when you relax and mix up your intonation. When she talked about struggling to use pork chops to eat noodle soup, meaning chopsticks, of course, she laughed so hard she snorted, even though she was frustrated at mixing up her words. It was impossible not to laugh along with her.

Samantha, another contributor to this book known for her silliness, brought her dad to work for a father-daughter day. Here's her hysterical story:

"Most of the other women at our company's uptown headquarters were bosses who sat in soundproofed, private, glass offices by the windows. I was a quiet underling, working in a sea of male co-workers in one of the cubicles separated by six-foot dividers. After observing my colleagues' brutal pranks on one another, I became even more reserved until Dad accidentally yanked me out of my comfort zone.

"He made an unforgettable impression on father-daughter day when he followed me into the copier room, which was open on both sides. It didn't occur to me to remind him that everyone in the surrounding room could hear our conversation. 'What's taking you so long?' he loudly asked, forgetting we lacked privacy. 'It's been ages since you went on a date, and there are all these great men out there. I want you to find a husband, Sweetheart. Why don't you just pick one?!'"

Samantha rolled her eyes as she told me, "I instantly crossed my arms in an emphatic 'STOP TALKING!' motion and mouthed, 'Shhhhh!' But the damage was done. You could have heard a feather drop on that hardwood floor as I left the copier room, with my father following closely behind me. I looked down as I felt the heat of 39 sets of eyes on me, waiting for a reaction. We had only walked a few steps when a wave of uproarious laughter broke the deafening silence. All I could do was crack up with my colleagues as I put my arm around Dad and yanked him toward the exit door. When we returned after lunch, my co-workers treated Dad like a rock star and invited him to join their social outings over the next few days. I don't believe any of them ever looked my way with serious romantic interest, but I saw their unleashed delight in getting intel on me for punchlines. Like it or not, I became an easy target, and, just as expected, I was pranked repeatedly after that day.

"It was a relief to discover their horseplay wasn't as cruel as I feared. Believe it or not, laughing at their twisted humor eventually caused me to feel sisterly camaraderie toward several of those clowns. The surprise effect of being let in on their jokes, even when the jokes were on me, made teamwork easier."

Samantha explained that she eventually became less uptight and even started to make wisecracks of her own in the office, which were well received. Over time, she gained confidence and began to expect listeners to laugh at her jokes. Samantha explained that developing her sense of humor had been a lot like training for a marathon—except instead of running. She just had to run her mouth!

Gestalt theory raises questions about how Samantha's perception shaped her reality. She said she began to believe she had a gift for amusing punchlines that would be well received, even though her wit was, in this author's opinion, drier than the Sahara Desert. Samantha's assumption that she had learned to become funny could explain why a jury member might believe he saw something that never happened. In the same way, you might have viewed a painting featuring train tracks that appear to vanish into the horizon. Sometimes we see what we expect to see, and what we expect to see is not the reality.

Even in dire circumstances, our brains can find the underlying humor, and we can discover the untapped potential for light relief *if we commit to looking for it*. For example, you could attend live comedy shows and consider joining a comedy workshop to improve your comedic timing. Or you could create notes on your smartphone when you hear funny one-liners to keep quips at your fingertips.

The headline here is to make finding your funny side a serious goal. With enough practice, you'll be juggling jokes and slipping on banana peels like a seasoned pro.

Chapter 15

CAN YOU AFFORD THOSE OVER-THE-KNEE GO-GO BOOTS?

SYNOPSIS:

According to my longtime friend and accountant, Rose, "Sophisticated people think about the comfort, practicality, and value they're getting for each dollar they spend instead of making frivolous purchases. Although an occasional treat is important to maintaining your overall well-being, remember that a $4 cup of coffee four times a week will cost you nearly $1,000 a year."

Dad used to play a game where he predicted who would purchase my mother's art at her out-of-town exhibits. He said, "If a man walks up to your mom's exhibit wearing heavy gold chains and flashy clothing, he's less likely to pull out his wallet and buy a painting than the less showy guy. The buyer often wears simple khaki pants and a casual denim shirt or a T-shirt. People with discretionary income generally don't make a show of wealth. They're discreet and have nothing to prove."

Looking back, I suspect my father was suggesting that I tone down my look: striped bell-bottoms, tie-dyed, batwing sweatshirts, and over-the-knee, white, zippered go-go boots. However, he humored my love for outlandish fashion statements and used to say, "Well, my stars, that's a memorable outfit." Years later, with a little maturity under my belt, I began to respect my father's diplomacy and his good eye. I should never have matched striped bell bottoms with a tie-dyed, batwing sweatshirt and go-go boots. A more fashion-forward pairing would have been a sleek, fitted, metallic puffer jacket and simple, platform Mary Jane pumps with big bows.

As Rose also told me, "If you have to worry about whether you can afford over-the-knee go-go boots, the answer is 'no,' you cannot afford them." She teaches her female clients that "improving your finances will greatly enhance your self-confidence." Rose was a bookkeeper when we met. Over the last decade, I've seen her earn her accounting license, and soon, she will be the new owner of her large and growing accounting firm. Her mantra is, "Taking care of your bills requires knowing what your bills are."

After creating a budget for living in Colorado, I did a self-audit to ensure I remained aware of my spending habits. My protective accountant encouraged me to go through credit card statements with a yellow highlighter. "When's the last time you checked all the app subscriptions you're paying for?" she asked.

"Is it possible that you're being auto-billed by even one company without using their services? Do you have bundled insurance for your home and your car?" She reminded me that small, pain-free ways to save do add up, just as "a stack of nickels saved soon becomes a dollar." In Rose's words, conducting a self-audit is like "a treasure hunt to find hidden money—except instead of pirates, you have receipts, and instead of a treasure map, you have a spreadsheet that makes you question your spending choices."

Simple ways that I've followed her direction by cutting my bills include:

- Adding a light-filtering film over my windows, which saves the furniture from sun damage and lowers my power bill;
- Purchasing cellular blinds made from a fabric that traps cold or hot air;
- Disconnecting electronics when not in use to avoid phantom energy costs; and,
- Buying generic medications.

I once met a man who made his living by auditing customers' bills and taking half the savings for his one-time payment. Like my accountant, saving money was his obsession. His eyes sparkled with excitement when he talked about reviewing utility bills, phone plans, home repair warranties, fitness club memberships, and grocery receipts.

What are your hobbies? Is anyone making money from them? Can one of your hobbies become a lucrative career? Is there a service that you already give away for free to friends or a product that you make that you could sell as a new business? There is always demand for entrepreneurship, but it will be easier to sell certain products at certain times. My friend who makes guitars has been selling them like hotcakes in recent years to people who want an economical pastime. I also remember meeting a store clerk who proudly told me he was on his last day of employment and would be leaving to open a used bicycle shop. Another entrepreneur I admire is my college student neighbor, who does in-home dog grooming.

Mama told me a story about her enterprising friend, Berthalee, a character who hid a small pistol in her lacy, V-neck chiffon camisole. My parents said they knew Berthalee and her husband for years before they realized they were wealthy. This couple had sold their furniture store in a recession to buy a pizza restaurant. According to my mother, they were humble people who had made enough money when inflation was high to start afresh and build an entirely new business. They also opened a catering business to diversify their income. After retiring, they gave all 11 grandchildren a pizza shop. Mama said this couple seemed blissfully happy and quoted Bertha as saying that, "Growing their income had become a fun game."

Several single GGs told me that dating a significantly older man can be challenging when it comes to financial freedom. They shared the view that many men over 60 are looking for a nurse or a purse. The battle cry of my survey group was the desire to avoid having to live a humble lifestyle just to finance an inattentive, lazy old bum who sits in his lounge chair and barks, "What's for dinner?"

Chapter 16

THE DAZZLING DANCE OF BODY AWARENESS

SYNOPSIS:

There are plenty of affordable ways to get some exercise. Enlisting an accountability partner can make it easier to show up for an early morning walk around the block or a quick hike. And the benefits for your physical and mental health are huge. Turbulence in life is inevitable, but exercise will help you to banish anxiety and approach confrontations with a peaceful demeanor, earning you respect and positively affecting how others relate to you.

The latest online exercise programs, addressed in this chapter, can help you glide through the room as you build a connection to your body while developing graceful movements and sexy muscle tone.

A strength and exercise regime can lift your mood and help prevent cardiovascular disease, cancer, and type 2 diabetes.[13] Obviously, you'll also want to be able to tie your shoes and zip the back of your dresses when you're old. There are the aesthetics to consider too: Loose skin on your legs, arms, and tummy can disappear faster with an enchanting routine that motivates you to keep working. Are you ready to think of housework and standing in long lines as a mini vacation?

I try to stay active and believe in cross-training. That means mixing up routines with little or no equipment, including running, walking flights of stairs at a fast clip, and yoga. Believing that stretching regularly could improve my concentration, I accepted my friend Audrey's invitation to join her for a sunrise walk around the lake near my home.

"This wondrous place is only minutes from my place? Are you serious?" I asked with delight. I had lived at my residence for more than two years and didn't realize this lake, with a magnificent Rocky Mountains backdrop, was just around the corner. It's amazing what you can learn about your surroundings when you make friends with an athletic neighbor.

I gave her the nickname, alluring Audrey for her humanitarian efforts and glamorous fashion sense. She met her husband at a Halloween party. Apparently, Audrey wasn't wearing much when they first locked eyes. According to him, her hair was wrapped in a white towel, and she had on a white bathrobe and a come-hither smile that mesmerized him from across the crowded room. He said they didn't talk for more than a minute or two at first, which made sense given that he was dripping in blood and dressed as a vampire.

---

13 According to a December 27, 2023 CDC article, "Physical Activity and Your Weight and Health," physical activity can reduce your risk of type 2 diabetes, several forms of cancer, heart disease, arthritis pain, osteoporosis, stroke, and high blood pressure as well as improving your ability to get a restful night's sleep.

Here's a fun fact: Many hopelessly romantic fashionistas, including those who've dressed up like Audrey Hepburn's character in Breakfast at Tiffany's for Halloween parties, refuse to believe that the beloved, glamorous heroine of the movie may have been an upscale call girl. It's so easy to adore Holly Golightly because she is playful, vulnerable, romantic, and mysterious. However, this classic movie's plot showed that she relied on wealthy men for financial support.

Although she looks like a movie star, my Audrey gets more recognition for her efforts to help others than for her stunning beauty. Every time we go walking, we're stopped by someone for whom she has conducted a wedding ceremony. Audrey is a pastor and missionary who also created a greeting card line using spiritual messages over brightly-colored, abstract paintings.

I've enjoyed her creative observations about the changing early morning light on the water lilies floating along Quail Lake. For instance, she recently stated, "It feels like we're walking into one of Claude Monet's paintings."

When she's not working as a minister or artist, she stays busy doing landscape gardening. Audrey has called my attention to tall cottonwoods and ponderosa pines surrounding us that I might otherwise have missed during our quick escapes into nature. Although a double loop around the lake is about a two-mile walk, it's easy to forget we're exercising. No wading or swimming is allowed, but it's fun to look out for kayakers, runners, dogs walking their owners, and fishermen looking to reel in catfish, wipers, crappie, and pike.

When I'm not hiking, prancing around my kitchen while humming aloud to classic ballet ballads holds tremendous appeal. After being snowed in and housebound a few times, I purchased an inexpensive, free-standing barre and enrolled in an online ballet class.

Fortunately, in-person training can be affordable when you subsidize lessons with free online instructional videos and books from your public library. Whether you choose individual, group, online, or one-on-one classes, you can become more agile than you ever thought possible. Furthermore, you'll learn to view classic performances, such as *Swan Lake* and *The Nutcracker*, with a more sophisticated understanding and appreciation.

I realize a nearly six-foot-tall female with grey roots and large peaches who has had bunion surgery is not your typical candidate for classical dance. But ballet is now my favorite exercise. Gracefully commanding more space can help you come across as a more confident person. You don't want to be the shrinking violet wilting away in the corner of the room. Self-assurance is all about delivery: Be the sunflower who skillfully stretches out her beautiful petals with her head held high.

It's easy to feel fancy when listening to classical music and dancing in cute little over-the-knee leggings and darling pink ballet slippers. Ballet has historically been thought of as a high-brow art that you begin in grade school and start to master in early adulthood. But the rules for participation in this art form have changed. Now there are new, flexible programs available for more mature beginners. Golden dames may be performing at your city's next student dance recital, and seeing their balance and poise can feel empowering. Try watching a few classic ballet-themed movies and picture yourself joining the world of glamorous silk and tulle costumes, beautifully braided hair buns, and romantic classical music. Dancing around your kitchen will get your heart pumping and send your mood soaring as emotions cycle through your body. And instruction doesn't have to be intimidating; the idea is to enjoy participating by modifying classic moves to make them accessible so you can perform at your best.

Envision defying gravity, as you sail through the air toward your dreams. Imagine that your spine is connected to your arms, like a horizontal brace. With your arms held straight to your side, like wings, with elegant hands stretching out at the end, your mind will lift off. Within a year, after consistent workouts, you may feel like you're learning to fly.

Furthermore, learning to spot adaptions that many experienced adult ballerinas are making can reinforce the liberating recognition that it's okay to do your best without demanding perfection. You'll also have the opportunity to catch up with friends if you choose to make outgoing calls with a hands-free earpiece while doing barre practice from home.

An additional side benefit may be learning to speak French, the language of ballet. When my teacher got pregnant, she sat in a chair and called out ballet positions from flashcards with definitions handwritten in French. In no time, instead of cooking "beef stew," I wanted to create *boeuf bourguignon*, and I discovered that *le petit dejeuner* is generally the most affordable meal to try if you want to sample French cooking. If you can afford the treat, visit an authentic French restaurant for strawberry breakfast crêpes or French toast while wearing a tailored blazer and a bright red beret.

After exercise, it can be a relaxing experience to take a warm bath in the evening before moisturizing every inch of your body, especially if you live in a dry climate. Your older self will thank you! After ensuring your skin is buttery soft, pick a pair of pretty, freshly laundered pajamas or a heavenly, silky negligee as another sensual reward for a challenging workout. After doing pliés every night for a few months—bending your knees while opening your arms like a butterfly's wings—take a long look at your dramatically improved body in front of a full-length mirror.

The cinematographer I interviewed explained that she "likes to focus her eyes on her body like a camera lens to maximize the good parts." This GG proudly wears short shorts without shame and noted, "I could negatively critique my pancake butt and thin, little ankles as genetically defective. But it makes me happy to see my sculpted calves and firm backside looking fierce in a pencil skirt."

Another body-positive contributor, a stylist, told me that even after a tragic accident, she likes to strut her stuff in a rhinestone-encrusted, fringed miniskirt. Soleil noted that she doesn't remember much after crashing her motorcycle face-first into a concrete wall on the highway.

"I woke up in the hospital with my husband of 26 years sitting beside me, holding my hand," she recounted. "We've come a long way since then. I had 49 stitches from my belly button to my hip. Today, I have a job I love as a country and western fashion trendsetter. Every time I remember the incident—spending a week in the ICU, 12 more days in the hospital and a few weeks in rehab—I thank God for my incredible life. You have no idea how much I appreciate the ability to enjoy country music concerts with my sweet man. Seeing the joy in his eyes when I mirror his steps before he twirls me around in my sparkling, fringed miniskirts and flutter-sleeve tops makes all my torturous rehab work worth the effort." Soleil explained that music is one of her best medicines and that when she looks at her scar, she is prone to "crying with joy."

"No woman should let anyone tell her she's too old or ugly to take pride in her body," she added. "Would you like to see the male and female yellow warblers I had tattooed over my scar?" Before I could say "yes," Soleil turned sideways and rolled down her leggings to show me the most beautiful artwork I'd ever seen. "These birds are happily perched on a wildflower stalk that covers my gorgeous scar. It helps me remember how important it is to count every day of good health as a blessing."

Meeting with Soleil had served as a poignant reminder: There is always someone with personal struggles worse than our own; struggles that we may never experience or fully comprehend. After our visit, I felt overwhelming gratitude for the breathtaking mountain sunset view on my drive home.

Chapter 17

BOOST YOUR PRODUCTIVITY AND SLAY DISTRACTIONS

SYNOPSIS:

Are you desperately in need of more free time to relax? This chapter teaches you how to turn on your warrior mode for more effective time management. Distractions can be defined as repetitive routines that don't bring you joy and might be disruptive. Practice blurring the line between critical performance and pleasure as you reclaim your calendar. Why live like an exhausted workhorse when you can become a playful, prancing pony?

STEP 1: Organize your learning so it doesn't distract.

One of the younger GG contributors suggested creating online bookmarks that you drop into folders on your desktop. This hipster said her process for staying digitally organized enables her to focus on critical tasks at hand and enjoy reading the articles later when she can relax.

Steal this trick for your old-school printed magazines. Rip out articles and leave them in a "read me later" folder. Now, circle back in a few days and enjoy guilt-free reading pleasure.

STEP 2: Try a social media and news detox.

If you're even slightly social media savvy, you've learned that likes and comments require returned likes and comments to sustain positive online feedback. Unfortunately, commenting thoughtfully on your friends' posts can quickly become a bottomless pit of lost time. Do you really want to lose this valuable real estate on your calendar to virtual interactions when you can spend the same time visiting beloved friends in person?

Remember that a social media detox can create more interest in your content. Furthermore, social media apps may push your posts if you take a break now and then. At a minimum, start posting and interacting on the same day and at the same time every week. This is an easy way to train others to look for your new photos and videos and a simple shortcut to spending less time at your computer.

Likewise, it's easy to get depressed these days after watching too much negative news. By taking a week off from watching stressful television, you can focus more on self-care.

STEP 3: Silence phone messages and notifications when you have tasks that require focus.

Have you trained friends and family to contact you when it's easier to talk? If you haven't already, spend two minutes researching computer settings that will allow you to temporarily stop phone calls and text interruptions.

STEP 4: Ease into the weekend.

Ideally, your most challenging tasks should be assigned on Mondays and Tuesdays so that your work week becomes easier as you approach the weekend.

If you need more social interaction, Friday might be a great designated "treat day" to meet for food and drinks with friends before gliding into a chill Saturday vibe. You could also plan to meet with customers in person or enjoy seeing a friend over lunch at the end of your week. Obviously, you'll want to run errands during times of the day when you know you'll miss heavy traffic. While you're being generous with yourself, you could occasionally plan to stop work by 4 pm to say goodbye to the hassles of rush hour.

STEP 5: Find a way to make repetitive tasks pleasant.

Think of friends and family visiting as a bell that signals that it's time to clean up your act. Instead of dreading the preparation for entertaining guests, look forward to the motivation it gives you to tidy and organize, as well as the reward of seeing your loved ones.

Buying groceries can become more enjoyable if you build meals around your new herb garden's harvest. Remember to shop early in the week when you'll miss the crowd. And if you can find time to download a grocery store app, you'll be astonished at the money you can save.

Washing and folding clothes can be a treat if you earmark these tasks for a day and time of the week when you can also listen to your favorite podcasts. Another way to turn laundry day into a satisfying experience is to multitask by returning calls. Make it a habit to pop in your earbuds before you start on your chores.

Consider buying a robot vacuum when they go on sale. Watching an electric assistant dust your entire home faster and more effectively than you can is a gratifying experience, especially if you live in the mountains and suffer from a dust allergy.

Creating a freshly brewed cup of coffee takes just a few minutes in the morning, but a small electric grinder can save time and pay for itself because ground beans cost more than whole beans. Furthermore, these handy gadgets can upgrade your daily ritual by enabling you to enjoy the intoxicating aroma of fresher coffee. If presentation matters to you, consider investing in an electric milk frother. Coffee comes with sticker shock these days, but it's surprisingly easy to draw foam hearts on your own cup of joe. And don't forget how quickly these savings can add up, making a membership to a wholesale club for groceries and household goods look affordable.

As for taking vitamins, save time by dropping tablets and capsules into your daily green smoothie.

People who look after their bodies are treated to a bottomless pit of advantages in life. Another intelligent beauty automation that can save your choppers from expensive, time-consuming dental procedures is to stock up on mouthwash and toothpaste brands that re-mineralize and strengthen tooth enamel.

STEP 6: Give your workspace more firepower.

Do you have a mobile computer stand to save you from backaches? The newest, industrial-style metal stands are stylish and far more affordable than spine doctors' visits.

A fellow dog lover stated, "When I lived with two and a half people in a 698 square foot condo, I used a lightweight, three-panel corkboard room divider to create a private workstation. I say two and a half people because our dog didn't realize he wasn't human. Noise-canceling headphones were a lifesaver for eliminating the sound of his squeaky toys."

If you've decided to return emails or do some work from a café or other location away from home or the office, consider purchasing a laptop camera cover. A removable screen that reduces eye strain can be another tool to make it more challenging for a rogue to hack your computer.

Protecting your peepers is also critical to working smarter because you only have one set. If you wear glasses, you can postpone eyesight loss and the need for new glasses by setting timers that remind you to look away from your computer screen regularly. In addition, it could be helpful to turn on the night mode setting to reduce eye strain and blue light exposure.

You'll also want to keep a large water bottle or pitcher prominently displayed and within easy reach. Drinking enough H2O is critical to hydrating your eyes.

STEP 7: Stick it to your daily tasks.

By now, automating your schedule has become so easy that you've started making a game out of guessing how much you can accomplish every day.

Need another way to make finishing your household chores easier? Put motivational stickers on the walls to bring pleasure to your inner child. One GG's backup hard drive has a sticker that says, "Don't give up."

Besides developing a sticker habit, scribbling down notes about your top three daily victories can be an inexpensive way to propel yourself forward. It's important to celebrate small wins. Mentally reviewing your successes for the day can revitalize your sense of optimism, provide perspective on your progress, and motivate you to attack larger goals.

Post your list of wins on your fridge so that you don't forget what you've achieved.

STEP 8: Track your losses.

How often have you either forgotten where you parked your car or been late to important meetings in the last three months? If the answer is more than once, dropping a smart device tracker in your glove compartment, purse, or suitcase can save you stress. You could also use an app on your computer that plays a ringtone when your phone is lost or stolen.

Nancy creates documentation and user manuals for tech products for a living. She told me that when she absentmindedly left her phone at her tailor's shop in Los Angeles a few years ago, the tailor was walking down Pico Street, looking for a lunch spot, before she realized her phone was missing.

Nancy said she "raced back to his store only to see a "'Back in an hour' sign on his door." Then she remembered that her computer had a tracker app. This modern-day digital detective raced down the street and followed him into an outdoor café, where he was seated calmly, eating a meatball sandwich. She told me they laughed when he handed over her phone.

STEP 9: Plan a monthly "me day."

You owe it to yourself to create time for micro-breaks, self-care dates, and mental health days. Micro-breaks mean taking a few minutes out of the day to practice yoga or meditate. If you work from home, you might want to refrigerate a small spray bottle of water to refresh your face. A quick spritz and a snack with a cold glass of H2O can give your energy levels a boost. Whether you'd rather spoil yourself with an extended lunch or make a date for tennis, enjoy the ability to goof off for a few hours at least once or twice a month.

Let's review the steps to becoming more productive and eliminating distractions:

STEP 1:   Organize your learning so it doesn't distract.

STEP 2:   Try a social media and news detox.

STEP 3:   Silence phone messages and notifications when you have tasks that require focus.

STEP 4:   Ease into the weekend.

STEP 5:   Find a way to make repetitive tasks pleasant.

STEP 6:   Give your workspace more firepower.

STEP 7:   Stick it to your daily tasks.

STEP 8:   Track your losses.

STEP 9:   Plan a monthly "me day."

On a final note, if the way you pay the bills makes you miserable start quietly researching other professions. New technology has dramatically changed our lives over the last few years. Instead of worrying about how it's become more challenging to make a living in your chosen profession, learn about new ways to branch out into an exciting side hustle that could eventually become your primary source of income.

Chapter 18

FOR THOSE WHO CARE ABOUT SOMEONE WITH ADHD

SYNOPSIS:

Trixie, the tech whiz, said to me, "I hope that one day, I will find a supportive community of friends who accept me for me, exactly the way I am. My ADHD can be a gift."

Reading this chapter could allow you to be that compassionate person for those with ADHD in your life. For medical questions about ADHD (attention deficit hyperactivity disorder), help connecting with like-minded people, and answers to questions about medications, please read updated research and look at the work of the preeminent experts on this topic: Dr. William Hallowell and Dr. John J. Ratey. Their book *Driven to Distraction* has sold more than 18 million copies. Hallowell and Ratey have set themselves apart from other experts by sharing an unusually optimistic outlook regarding managing ADHD.

Trixie wrote the following short letter. Maybe you know another woman dealing with similar issues, or maybe that woman is you.

I wrote this letter to help women like me find supportive communities and rethink how they see themselves. I am misunderstood but gifted, and my so-called "disability" is part of what makes me special. Yet, every day feels like a battle against a world that often overlooks the beauty of my differences.

One would expect my extraordinary imagination to be an asset, but the truth is, my creative thoughts can spiral into chaos, leaving me feeling trapped in a whirlwind of ideas that I can't control. I've been told a zillion times that I get "over-enthusiastic" about subjects that excite me and that I'm an "overthinker." These labels sting. You know what? I am over being criticized and agonizing over feeling like I'm constantly a step behind in a race I never agreed to run.

It doesn't make sense to look at my ADHD as a "curse." What other people might see as me being "distracted" has often been me picking up on clues to life-or-death details that they missed. I possess specialized professional skills and take pride in helping people navigate challenges they can't solve alone. I've given clients insights that have saved them thousands of dollars, as well as time and stress. But people who don't understand my superpowers still frequently dismiss my comments as long-winded "bird walks." The irony is painful.

I know my racing thoughts and lengthy chatter can overwhelm listeners, but sometimes, it feels like I'm juggling fiery torches while walking backward in circles. I wish you could try and understand my struggles with perfectionism, depression, and loneliness. I wish you cared enough to see the person behind the label. Partners, friends, family members, and teachers have hurt my feelings with phrases like "cut to the chase" or "can you just get to the point?" Each dismissal feels like a physical cut, deepening my sense of isolation. I've learned to shield myself from the sting of rejection, opting instead for the comfort of solitude. Being alone is easier than facing those who fail to respect my feelings and my worth as a human being.

The ADHD label can feel like a noose around my identity. If you can't see the glory in my unique perspective, step to the back of the line behind the rest of my haters. I deserve to be treated with respect, and I long for connections with people who celebrate my quirks instead of throwing the ADHD label in my face. I pray that one day, I will find a supportive community of friends who accept me for me, exactly the way I am.

Chapter 19

FEARLESSLY WALK THE WORK-LIFE TIGHTROPE

SYNOPSIS:

In the short letter below, Mindy, a home-based executive, shares her frustration with her lack of work-life balance. After reading her comments, take a moment to think about what self-care habits she could develop to improve her life. Then read the list of ideas that have helped other GGs who have walked in Mindy's shoes. This chapter also covers work-life balance for a caregiver.

My name is Mindy. I often find myself running behind, like a gerbil on a wheel of responsibilities. Every day feels like a juggling act, and I'm unsure how much longer I can keep it up. There's no time for fun and self-care. I love my partner, but the weight of our financial situation and the demands of my job create tension between us that feels increasingly hard to bridge.

I work long hours from home that often stretch into the evening. While I earn a decent salary, I'm living paycheck to paycheck. My partner makes less than I do, so I bear the brunt of our financial responsibilities. I'm constantly afraid that one unexpected bill—a medical emergency or a car repair—could send everything crashing down around us. I have no safety net, and the thought of being unprepared keeps me awake at night.

I feel isolated. While I have the luxury of working from home, I miss interaction with colleagues. My evenings are spent in solitude, cooking meals and cleaning the house, while my partner unwinds in front of the TV, seemingly oblivious to the emotional toll his attitude takes on me. He works hard all day, and I understand he's tired, but I wish he would share more responsibilities around the house. I'm left feeling like the only adult, managing chores and responsibilities while he drifts through the evening routine.

Self-care has become a distant memory because exhaustion overrides any motivation to prioritize my health. I'm resigned to quick meals and sporadic short walks around the neighborhood for exercise, and, as a result, my self-esteem has plummeted.

Social media doesn't help either. My life feels dull compared to the highlight reels I see online, and online posts chip away at my fragile self-worth.

I want to believe that life can be different and that I can balance my work and personal happiness, but I feel overwhelmed. I need to find a way to break free from this cycle—before it breaks me. The weight of my responsibilities is heavy, and I long for a life that feels lighter, more fulfilling, and less lonely.

Now that we have seen what life is like for Mindy, let's review some ideas that have worked for the GGs I've spoken to about work-life balance:

1. Set clear goals.

2. Create a morning routine.

3. Declutter your space.

4. Start a gratitude journal.

5. Limit social media or at least take a break.

6. Read daily.

7. Learn a new skill.

8. Network.

9. Exercise a minimum of 30 minutes every day.

10. Eat a healthy, balanced diet.

11. Practice mindfulness.

12. Establish boundaries.

13. Track your spending.

14. Volunteer.

15. Consider talking to a therapist.

16. Cultivate new relationships.

17. Limit computer time.

18. Plan repetitive weekly tasks.

19. Celebrate small victories.

More than one Guardian Gal™ mentioned the need to avoid social isolation and to cultivate diversity in your friendships. Too often, we lose track of our friends or even push them away. This can be for many reasons, including the following:

- Tuning out the world while focusing on a romantic partner.
- Going back to school or starting a challenging new job with extremely long hours.
- Financial inequities, which can cause friction.
- Physical or mental illness.
- Enjoying time with a new baby or grandbabies.
- The call to serve as a caregiver for sick parents, adult children, a romantic partner, or a best friend.

Although I've woven other women's narratives into my own experiences in this book, the following story about finding work-life balance as a caregiver is solely my personal contribution.

Make no mistake. I willingly volunteered to help my parents when they were in trouble, and I will always look back on the opportunity to assist them in their time of need as my greatest accomplishment in life. While I helped them, I never felt like I was doing a "job." It was a labor of love. Supporting them gave me an incredible sense of purpose. In retrospect, however, I realize I was unprepared for the long hours and stress overload. It was only after I developed thicker skin that I began to prioritize my own self-care.

Thankfully, I now understand the critical importance of avoiding social isolation. I've also realized that some close friends stop calling when it's your turn to ask for help. This knowledge has been a game-changer for me that has helped me find a new "normal" and feel more in control of my well-being. The following excerpt is from an article I wrote in 2020 for *Skidaway Island Neighbors Magazine*.

TAKE CARE OF THE CAREGIVER

I was never a parent until I served in that role as the primary caregiver for my own parents. When my physician firmly told me, "I won't see you as my patient anymore unless you call a care management service provider to help you care for your mom," my jaw dropped. I didn't want to lose Dr. Gaudry as my doctor and close friend. More importantly, I didn't want to lose my 82-year-old mother.

As I told Dr. Pam, Mama had recently fallen and busted her lip. When I looked at the bleeding gash, I felt paralyzed for the first time in my eight-and-a-half years as her primary caregiver. In the past, I've kept my head during crises. But the demands in this complex job had escalated, given Mom's new propensity for dizziness and falling. I was in over my head and exhausted from working 50 to 80 hours a week and being on call 24/7. I couldn't keep smiling and pretending everything was okay when I was this frightened.

I keep a diary to reduce depression. I hope this article will open the door for at least one other caregiver like me to reclaim her sense of joy and self-worth. That said, it's nearly impossible to share my personal life on a deep level because there's been no "me" for a long time.

I want my identity back.

The last thing Dr. Pam said was to "put on your own oxygen mask first and then help others." Per her advice, I called a caregiver service. It couldn't have been a coincidence that the first thing our family's new care management strategist said was, "Take care of yourself first so that you can take care of your mom."

What do the logistics look like? My mother doesn't have long-term care insurance, and the services I've helped her contract for could become cost-prohibitive. Still, we're creating a budget-friendly, tailor-made program featuring the following elements:

- Care management: Our registered nurse manager's first project will be to double-check that Mama receives the best insurance services at the best rates.
- Assistant caregivers: I look forward to taking a short weekly break.
- In-home physical therapy: This will help my mother regain balance and core strength.
- In-home, slow-paced yin yoga classes: These will improve her muscle tone, emphasizing meditation and stress relief.

I don't feel comfortable asking for so much help. Yet, if I've interpreted what the experts have told me correctly, it's not selfish to care for myself first. I'll need to put more thought into my personal mental and physical wellness. Hiring an assistant caregiver for a few hours a week is insufficient relief. I need oxygen too.

THE HAPPY UPDATE

I had expected to serve as my parents' primary caregiver for a few months, which turned into more than a decade. During that time, I dropped to my seventh-grade weight, had brain fog, began stuttering, and experienced trouble walking while barely holding down multiple full-time jobs.

As mentioned, after Dad abruptly died, Mom and I relocated from the Deep South to Colorado to get her access to emergency healthcare specialists. I was still recovering from a divorce when she passed away a couple of months after our cross-country move. Losing a parent the week before Christmas, during a blizzard, right after a divorce, and moving to a new state where you don't have a job or local friends does not make for a merry holiday season. I mostly stayed in bed snuggled up with a fleece blanket and our sweet puppy. I was grieving, scared, cold, and disconnected from my self-worth and sense of belonging.

The week after my mother passed, it wouldn't be an exaggeration to say that my sister, Jennifer, sometimes called me half a dozen times a day. She incessantly worried about me and the dog; the thought of us being snowed in with little food and flickering electricity in sub-freezing temperatures was too much for her. I begged her to stop making me talk because I felt humiliated by stuttering that came out of the blue, even when I wasn't nervous. But Jenny kept pestering me to text her the letters "POL" every day before noon. As she explained, this stands for "proof of life," the special weapons and tactical code for "I'm okay" in a survival emergency. My baby sister can be dramatic.

After a couple of weeks, Jen lightened up on the check-ins. The timeline remains fuzzy, but the power returned permanently at some point, and I started dressing in freshly laundered clothes. One day, I tucked the puppy into his wicker basket, and we headed outdoors for a bicycle ride to see purple wildflowers in bloom against the blue Southwestern sky. As I started unwinding from a loop tape of grief and worries, I vowed to build a beautiful new life. I started writing because, at the time, speaking was excruciating. The compassionate women who shared their confidential success stories for this book taught me an overdue lesson: Caring for others can give your life purpose, but learning how to accept help is just as important.

Chapter 20

COUNT YOUR BLESSINGS, NOT SHEEP

SYNOPSIS:

This chapter will help you take your daily gratitude practice to the next level. Your accomplishments are about to include going to bed at a reasonable time so that you'll wake up feeling refreshed and gorgeous.

Have you ever noticed that it's easier to wreck your car, have fuzzy thinking, age faster, and become ill when you don't sleep enough? There's also a direct correlation between the ability to feel attractive and happy and high-quality sleep. Your bedroom is sacred, and sleep is the fuel you need to slay the following day.

Here are some tips for a restful night:

- A strict no blue light and no social media policy for an hour before bedtime will strengthen your ability to close your eyes with a sense of peace.

- By conscientiously backing up important files to the cloud and an external hard drive, you'll be able to go to sleep without the worry of losing critical work if your computer crashes the next day.
- Before you get into bed, refill the emergency overnight grab bag beside your front door, checking that the flashlight underneath your bedside table is still charged and within easy reach. These days, wildfires, blizzards, flash floods, hurricanes, and tornadoes are genuine threats, and knowing you have everything you need within easy reach will allow you to sleep without anxiety. You could also hang a modest and comfy robe close to your bed in case you need to race out of the house in the middle of the night. Besides that, you can check a weather app every evening, making you less likely to get caught off guard by storms.
- Make your evening routine one of comfort and luxury so that you look forward to sleep. It's almost that time of day when you can escape to the pleasure of your elegant boudoir's cocoon of cool temperatures and darkness. First, you'll soak in a warm, muscle-relaxing bubble bath. Lying in the tub, you allow your breathing to slow as you release stressful thoughts and enjoy reflecting on little victories that help you remain confident that you're on track to achieving your biggest dreams.

Living a life of gratitude is critical for contentment as well as a good night's rest. You had a series of tiny wins today that show your life is steadily improving. You realize you're becoming a more peaceful person as you reach for the large glass of iced water beside your bath. It was a day worth celebrating by taking this time away from the hustle and bustle. Doing nothing but being present lets you reflect on simple, sweet pleasures.

You had a big grin on your face for an entire hour after passing the little, free neighborhood library at the end of your street. It was fun to catch a glimpse of a teenage girl sprinting away from the book stand, clutching your copy of *Moby Dick* tightly to her chest. You deposited this literary gem last week because you enjoy helping young people realize that building intellectual and ethical strength can help them navigate the world. Whenever you've seen this young lady around the neighborhood, she's always looked sad. Her severe acne problem must adversely affect her self-esteem, especially at that age. You struggled with debilitating acne as a teenager, too, so you feel her pain. She appears shy and doesn't usually walk confidently, but today, she looked full of delight.

Knowing that you inspired her joy motivates you to plan on dropping off additional books at the library so that more neighborhood kids can discover the joy of learning. Your hardcover treasures can lift others' spirits. You quietly and frequently do random acts of kindness and community service for the right reasons. No one has to know. Seeing how that innocent young girl appreciated your book was a sweet reminder that even small gestures for your fellow humans add meaning to life.

Although many unpleasant challenges lie ahead, you've begun treating each day more like a game. Instead of feeling locked into adverse circumstances, you're changing your mindset and attracting more blessings. Not long ago, you were constantly running late. But recently, you've spent more thoughtful time preparing for each day and left the house a few minutes earlier to greet the world. You've driven at an average speed instead of racing around and burning more fuel. Even the massive construction projects that have caused traffic jams around your city haven't dampened your good spirits. Instead of listening to the sounds of industrial equipment and beeping horns, you've been tuning in to foreign language tapes and picking up a few helpful phrases.

When you made a quick stop at a local market today and asked the owner for ingredients to make a stew, you felt a surge of accomplishment in explaining that you wanted to substitute turkey for chicken in your *pozole de pollo*. This sweet old man's big, toothy grin gave you the impression that he assumed Spanish was not your native language. But he clearly enjoyed your attempt to authentically connect with his culture. As you continue to relax in the warm bath water, you realize that improving your literacy has increased your ability to understand others, expanded your vocabulary, and enhanced your concentration and ability to focus. That's actually a series of *big* wins.

Just outside the Spanish grocery, you saw a couple of young children with their father, carefully studying a large clover patch. "Do you know the secret to spotting the lucky ones?" you casually asked. The young boy, who appeared to be about seven or eight, gleefully exclaimed, "*Mi hermana encontró un cuatro hoja!*" Despite barely knowing any Spanish, understanding that "cuatro" means "four" and noticing that this cutie was looking directly at his sister enabled you to take an accurate guess at the meaning of his words.

When you pointed toward two more lucky four-leaf clovers, those kids couldn't contain their excitement. It was delightful to see their serious expressions as you showed them how each leaf has a white triangle, making the extra leaf on the four-leaf clovers easy to spot.

Other small but happy moments today included enjoying the bright blue sky and sunny weather and the thrill of reading about your favorite local football player in the newspaper. You also noticed a full-page ad for an upcoming free health and wellness expo. Meeting like-minded neighbors interested in physical and mental well-being will be a pleasure. You've already got a busy schedule this Saturday, but you also know the value of pushing yourself to show up in the right place at the right time. You'll arrive at the expo early to walk the booths and meet community members; these connections will raise your odds of having more lucky opportunities.

While reading the newspaper does take time, it also gives you more to talk about with people from all walks of life. It's no coincidence that you've been able to easily converse with strangers recently about subjects that are interesting to them. Building a more extensive network of friends from different age groups and backgrounds has enabled you to get higher-quality referrals for everything from haircuts to home improvements. You've also noticed that intentionally meeting new people has helped lower your feeling of uncertainty in life, as well as your stress levels.

You relished today's quick video chat with an old friend who lives abroad. She asked her children to hop online to say hello. Wow! They've grown up so fast. It's comforting to see people you care about doing well. Although phone calls are still memorable, you push yourself to talk in person whenever possible for a more intimate experience.

Your friend and her family have invited you to visit them abroad when you can manage the trip. The truth is that, even if you never get to go, it feels lovely to be invited, and you *will* try to make it someday. A vacation could give you a breather from life, enabling you to temporarily forget your problems, while deepening bonds with people you love.

A side benefit of talking face-to-face was that you brushed your hair and refreshed your lipstick before hopping on the call. Paying a little more attention to your appearance is starting to pay off! It's not a coincidence that the days you've taken time to look your best frequently mark your favorite memories. Audrey Hepburn was right when she famously said girls who feel pretty are happier.

Before standing up from your bath and grabbing a freshly washed, fluffy towel, you anticipate the lavender scent of your soft pillows and the light breeze emanating from your window. You're sure you'll quickly drift off to sleep. You mentally pat yourself on the back for having the forethought to prepare treats for a quick breakfast as you finish that glass of water and rub lotion onto your arms, legs, and belly. Even in this dry climate, your pretty skin stays soft and youthful. Before grabbing earplugs and a satin face mask, you snack on sleep-inducing yogurt with a few slices of kiwi and a handful of almonds.[14]

You'll count your blessings instead of sheep tonight. Your final prayer of gratitude for today will include:

- Special thanks for the luxury of healthy, delicious food;
- The excellent fortune of interacting with fascinating people;
- Learning to see your life from the perspective of someone who *expects* to feel glamorous, lucky, and happy;
- And the pleasant feeling of quickly falling asleep now that you are happily exhausted.

---

14 Elliot, B. (January 17, 2024) The 9 Best Foods and Drinks to Have Before Bed, Healthline.com https://www. healthline.com/nutrition/9-foods-to-help-you-sleep

Chapter 21

OPEN THE FLOODGATES AND CELEBRATE YOUR JOURNEY

SYNOPSIS:

You've skyrocketed your productivity, simplified repetitive routines, and cut expenses. Prepare to breathe in courage as you exhale fierce joy and laughter. Life-changing opportunities are just around the corner.

Consistently successful individuals don't stumble upon greatness without intention. As you celebrate your journey, you've begun experiencing the world with a more playful attitude.

- You vacuum your home wearing a luxurious negligee.
- Flirting outrageously with an exotic, gorgeous stranger using the new foreign phrases you've recently learned feels natural. If you're in a serious relationship, this game seems otherworldly because that fantasy stranger is your real-life mate.

- Your wardrobe, just like your home décor, is pleasing, and you dress up with your pets in matching rock band T-shirts and bomber jackets.
- You take candle-lit bubble baths while listening to your favorite music and eating decadent red velvet cupcakes with chocolate sprinkles.
- You decorate and dress in sparkly rhinestones to celebrate the holidays.

CHEERS to developing the emotional resilience to navigate challenges and setbacks effectively!

CHEERS to continuous growth and lifelong learning!

And CHEERS to reinforcing your ability to uplift others!

- You've learned to defend your heart from those who bring harm, whether by design or accident. But you remember that it's impossible to fully know what devastating tragedies the person who intentionally or unintentionally hurts you has survived.
- You realize that your neighbor, who looks like she has every glittering thing in this world, may have suffered unbearable loss.
- You understand that you do not truly know your best friend's silent struggles because you don't walk in her shoes.

It's become second nature to liberally use the magical phrases "Please," "Thank you," "I appreciate you," and, most importantly, "I love you."

Epilogue

EVEN IN DARKNESS, YOU CAN STILL LEARN TO FLY

Back in Los Angeles, people-watching was a quick way to recharge. In Savannah, I took ferryboat rides to Hutchinson Island for coffee breaks because breathing fresh, waterfront air was exhilarating, and it was exciting to spot brown thrashers, chickadees, and ruby-throated hummingbirds. California and Georgia will always be close to my heart. Living in Colorado Springs wasn't originally part of my long-term plan, but this lifestyle is growing on me.

Mama and I made it a goal to visit the Rocky Mountains, which she nicknamed "The Top of the World." We wanted to see exotic wildlife, like bison and bighorn sheep. It's exciting when your picture of the future merges with reality. I thought my eyes were playing tricks on me the first time I saw a flying squirrel, and I've driven off the road numerous times to enjoy vast fields of sunflowers.

My mother was a lifelong artist who looked out of the window in her Colorado bedroom with childlike joy. A few weeks after she passed, I set an alarm and woke up early, slipping into her bed to catch a glimpse of what had once brought her joy. I needed to understand why, even though she had laid there all day for weeks, too sick to move, she still woke up early to see the sun rise.

As the dawn's rapidly changing light rose over what she had referred to as "my mountain," her hungry friend, the northern flicker woodpecker, returned. I'd never seen this greedy baby bird before. Instead of getting upset that he had feasted on breakfast outside the bedroom window, I enjoyed the big heart he chipped into our elm tree. His artwork continues to serve as a sweet reminder that *there is good in this world*.

Her little squirrel stopped by to visit me as well. He had a fluffier tail than I'd ever seen on any animal before, and he was clutching a large, green leaf in his mouth. "Squirrely Pie," as she loved to call him, appeared to be gliding over our fence while simultaneously balancing breakfast in his claws. I couldn't believe my eyes. There was *and is* so much wonder to discover.

I sincerely hope this book helps you feel less alone as you seek meaning in your life and joyfully search for four-leaf clovers and sunshine. Remember that, even in darkness, you can still learn to fly.

"FLY TOWARD FREEDOM"

Make no excuses for who you are.
Shut down doubters.
Reach high, and travel far.

It's time to hit the bullseye.
Claim the dream you believe.
Let go of your fears.
Take the leap of faith to achieve.

Pamper your soul and allow your heart to play.
Fly toward freedom,
And celebrate this happy great day®!

Focus your power,
And soar toward the sun.
Rediscover laughter.
Create a life that's more fun.

IT'S TIME TO LIVE YOUR DREAM!

GG Suzana

WANT MORE HAPPINESS IN YOUR EVERYDAY LIFE?

Join the Happy Great Day® community and unlock practical, wallet-friendly strategies to boost your well-being! I'm Suzana Ward, the author. I'm on a mission to uncover the secrets to a joyful life. And I'm sharing everything I learn from my amazing circle of Guardian Gals™ with you.

Don't miss out. Continue your journey!

Subscribers gain access to:

- Exclusive content and new "happiness hacks"
- Behind-the-scenes insights from the lives of fierce heroines who inspire bravery and self-love
- Contests to amazing prizes from the Book Swag Store!
- Plus, nominate your Guardian Gal™ to be a guest blogger or even a character in my next book.

Let's learn how to live more fulfilling lives together as we celebrate the strong women who empower us all! Visit www.happygreatday.com today.

Thank you for reading this book. If you're interested in footnotes, please contact the publisher through our website.

May your path be bright and your heart be light!

Here's to your success,

Suzana

ABOUT THE AUTHOR

In her darkest moments, Author and Fine Artist Suzana Ward thought God was punishing her. Looking back, she now realizes that the crushing personal losses which sent her spiraling into depression also gave her the insight for a remarkable lifestyle transformation. The joyful "Guardian Gals™" she researches for Happy Great Day® books, articles, blogs, and talks have taught Suzana to leave her comfort zone in pursuit of extraordinary dreams and grand adventures. When she's not sharing wallet-friendly ways to experience more laughter and luxury, she enjoys scenic mountain hikes; discovering off-the-beaten-path local churches; wearing outrageously big hats with knee-high turquoise cowboy boots; and getting lost in classic poetry. She is an avid dog lover, and a formidable pool shark.

www.ingramcontent.com/pod-product-compliance
Lightning Source LLC
Chambersburg PA
CBHW071303130626
46556CB00003B/1445